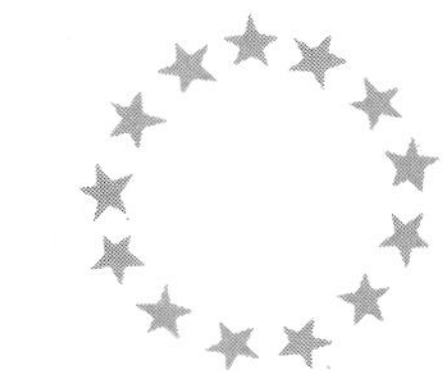

A FORGE OF
FREEDOM BOOK

0
50
100
200
MILES
N
W
E
S
Ticonderoga
N.H.
Portsmouth
Boston
Plymouth
NEW
YORK
Albany
MASS.
Hartford
CONN.
R.I.
Newport
Providence
New Haven
N.Y.
N.J.
New York City
PENNSYLVANIA
Trenton
Philadelphia
Burlington
Wilmington
Baltimore
Annapolis
DEL.
MD.
MD.
VIRGINIA
Richmond
Williamsburg
Jamestown
ATLANTIC OCEAN
NORTH CAROLINA
New Bern
Charlotte
Wilmington
SOUTH
CAROLINA
Charleston
GEORGIA
Savannah
The Thirteen Colonies
1763
RIKI

THE VIRGINIA COLONY

by

Elswyth Thane

CROWELL-COLLIER PRESS
Division of Macmillan Publishing Co., Inc.
New York
COLLIER MACMILLAN PUBLISHERS
London

Library of Congress Catalog Card Number: 69–16488

Macmillan Publishing Co., Inc., 866 Third Avenue, New York, N.Y. 10022
Collier Macmillan Canada Ltd.
Printed in the United States of America

4 5 6 7 8 9 10

PICTURE CREDITS

College of William and Mary, 72, 75; Colonial Williamsburg, 7, 10–11, 46–47, 52–53, 62, 78, 83, 110, 120; Culver Pictures, Inc., 3, 92, 106, 109; Historical Pictures Service—Chicago, 4, 5, 6, 15, 26, 32–33, 41, 65, 67, 115; National Park Service, 23; New York Historical Society, 18–19; State Historical Society of Wisconsin, 88–89; Virginia State Library, 9, 38, 48, 56–57, 61, 62, 85, 90, 94–95, 97, 103

COVER ILLUSTRATON: *Mount Vernon.*

To Florence Hanson
One of the Real Teachers

Contents

chapter 1

Columbus Discovers a New World

Everyone knows that Columbus discovered America in 1492. But it is interesting to learn that he was only looking for a new route to Asia. He did not know that America was there.

At that time the brightly colored silks and sweet spices and gold and silver jewelry which merchants brought back from China and the East Indies were very much admired in Europe. It was a dangerous journey for the traders. They had to bring the goods by caravans, which were long trains of loaded animals, on foot to the Mediterranean Sea, and they usually travelled by boat the rest of the way to Italy or Spain or France.

The savage Turks at the eastern end of the Mediterranean Sea often attacked the caravans and robbed them, and sold the traders into slavery. If the traders got as far as the boats, they were likely to be attacked by pirates in the Mediterranean.

Columbus had an idea that there was another way to reach Asia. He said that the earth was round, and if that was so, then he could sail westward from Europe and reach Asia by the back door. He was not the first man to have that idea, but he was the first to try to prove it.

In the beginning nobody would listen to him, or give him the money he needed for ships and crews. Finally the King and Queen of Spain were willing to give him three little ships for the voyage. Among his crews there were many ignorant men who still believed that the earth was flat. They were afraid that if they sailed too far westward from Europe they were sure to drop off the edge of the Atlantic Ocean into nothingness and would never be heard of again.

Nevertheless, Columbus sailed from the port of Palos in Spain on August 3, 1492, with ninety men divided among his three little ships. After they had been at sea for nine weeks, his unwilling crews were all frightened and wanted to turn back. Just in time they sighted land, on October 12, a date which is now celebrated in America as Columbus Day. Columbus thought he had arrived at one of the islands on the fringe of Japan, but he had come to the West Indies instead.

No one is sure just where Columbus first set foot on land in the New World. It was probably on one of the islands we now call the Bahamas in the Caribbean Sea. His surroundings were not quite what he expected, but he collected a few weapons and some pearls and gold ornaments from the natives to take back with him. He called the Caribbean natives Indians, because he still thought he was somewhere in Asia near Calcutta, India, and they have been called that ever since.

When he returned safely in March, 1493, to the same Spanish port from where he had sailed eight months before, everyone was very surprised to see him alive, and they

Christopher Columbus

made much of him at the Spanish Court. At that time in the world's history his voyage was a triumph which can be compared to our early astronauts' first orbits around the earth in space—he had not fallen off the edge of the Atlantic Ocean, and he had found land out there.

The Spanish King was not satisfied with the value of the cargo Columbus brought back. He sent him out again on other voyages, which took him to places we now call Puerto Rico and Santo Domingo. But in the West Indies Columbus found no oriental rugs or Eastern spices and silks like those the caravans brought back overland. He thought he was a failure. In his disappointment he finally returned home to Italy and died there in poverty. He never knew he had discovered a whole new world. He had never stood on what we now think of as American soil. But he had, as he said himself, "opened the gates" for other voyagers to come.

A great many explorers made the long Atlantic voyage during the next hundred years. They found wonderful native temples full of gold and silver treasure in Central America and Mexico. But it was nearly one hundred years after Columbus that an Englishman named Sir Francis Drake sailed around the world and back to England. He

Columbus's ships, the Niña, Pinta, *and* Santa Maria

had to go down around the tip of South America and across the Pacific and Indian oceans in his ship called the *Golden Hind*. On the way he landed in Peru and other South American countries, where he robbed the temples and the natives and carried the treasure back to Queen Elizabeth I.

There were already Spanish settlements in what we now call Florida and in Central America before England ever tried to start a colony in America. It had meanwhile got its name from an Italian sea captain, Amerigo Vespucci, who was the first man to assert that the new land was a continent itself, and not just a fringe of Asia

One of Queen Elizabeth's courtiers named Sir Walter Raleigh was fooled by the gold and silver from the native

The landing of Columbus (from an old manuscript)

Sir Walter Raleigh

temples and dreamed of making a great fortune in America. Raleigh sent out several expeditions which were supposed to set up a colony on the shore of what we now call North America, but the men died or were killed by the Indians, and they found nothing of any real value.

Queen Elizabeth named the new country Virginia, and its early boundaries included land which we now think of as North Carolina and even Maryland and Pennsylvania. Nobody had any idea of the size of the continent which lay between the Atlantic and the Pacific oceans, and thought it might be about two hundred miles wide, instead of three thousand.

The first colony which lasted any time at all was at Roanoke, which lay below the line which divides Virginia from North Carolina today. But it was all called Virginia then. This was the first party which included women, and a child was born there at Roanoke in August, 1587—the first English child to be born in the New World. They named her Virginia Dare.

The ships had run short of supplies during the long voyage from England. The Indians did not attack the colony

King James I

at first, but the settlers were afraid to depend on them for food. They decided to send a ship back to England to load up with more tools and provisions. Their leader went with it, a man named John White, who was the grandfather of Virginia Dare. Long as the voyage was, they expected him to get back to Roanoke before winter.

He was delayed in England, and by the time he reached Roanoke again, the whole colony had disappeared. He was obliged to return to England without knowing what had become of the people he had left at Roanoke. We do not know to this day whether they were killed by the Indians or starved to death. A great many stories have been told about the fate of the baby called Virginia Dare, but it remains a mystery.

Queen Elizabeth died and James I came to the throne in England. He also believed that great riches could be found in America, and he encouraged more colonists to set out on the dangerous adventure.

chapter 2

A Fort Called Jamestown in Virginia

A few days before Christmas in 1606, some little ships were outfitted by the London Company, which had been formed in England to put up money for a new settlement in Virginia. It was a commercial proposition only, and the Company expected big returns. The captain of the best ship was named Christopher Newport. Among his passengers there were several men of good family and high connections, and there was also a soldier-adventurer named John Smith. He had been in several wars, and had had many narrow escapes, and he was a much better man for the undertaking than most of the others in the party. They looked down on him, however, and there were quarrels and hard feelings during the long voyage.

In April of 1607 Newport's ships weathered a storm which drove them into the lower end of the Chesapeake Bay. They passed through what we now call Hampton Roads and came to the mouth of a wide river which they named

Captain John Smith

the James, after their King. They sailed up the river and found a place where the water was deep enough to let them tie up their ships to the big trees growing on the shore. There was an island in the river, which was joined to the mainland by a narrow neck of land called a peninsula. When they landed and walked inland from the shore, they found beautiful spring flowers and wild strawberries. They were weary of their crowded quarters on board the ships and decided to settle there on the island, which they called Jamestown.

They elected a man named Edward Wingfield as their president, though he was not a good choice. Their parson, whose name was Robert Hunt, nailed a board between two trees to rest the Bible on, stretched a sailcloth awning above it, and read the Episcopal service every day and twice on Sundays.

The settlers at once began to cut down trees for logs so that they could build a fort with a palisade around it. The palisade was a tall fence made of logs stood on end and fastened together with no open spaces between. The whole thing was in the shape of a triangle with the widest side towards the river. It had a strong gate in the middle of that

side. At the top of each point of the triangle they set a small cannon, and there were smaller entrances under each cannon. The triangle enclosed about an acre of ground, and there was room inside it for a few small houses built of logs and roofed with mud and thatch, which was made of rushes or reeds. They also built a little church and a storehouse of the same materials. They cleared some land and planted English wheat.

While this work was going on, Smith and Newport led a

The Jamestown settlers built their fort in the shape of a triangle

small exploring party up the river as far as where Richmond stands today. They passed several Indian villages along the banks. The Indians who lived in them seemed friendly and the white men were careful not to offend them. The Indians were pleased to accept such simple gifts as pins, looking-glasses, cheap beads, and little bells. This was a tribe of the Algonquins. Their chief was called the Powhatan.

When Captain Newport and Smith returned to the landing place after their trip up the river, they found that the men they had left behind to build the fort had been attacked by a different tribe of Indians, who were not as friendly as the ones they had met on the river banks. These Indians had hidden in the tall grass which grew at the edges of the island on the landward side and shot their silent, stone-tipped arrows into the fort and the clearing. After several of the English had been wounded by the arrows, they all retreated to their ships which were lying off the shore, and were safe there. Cannon fire from the decks frightened the savages away. The Powhatan's friendly Indians offered their protection from the other Indians and suggested that the white men had better cut down the tall grass which had hidden their attackers.

The fort was finished by the middle of June. The settlers made a farewell dinner on shore for Newport and his crews. The next day he started back to England with two of his ships. He left the smallest one for the colonists to use in exploring the river and shoreline. He took back with him as cargo a load of fine timber, some worthless rocks which he hoped contained gold, and an herb called sassafras which was used as medicine for fevers and also in making perfumes. Today we find it as a flavoring for old-fashioned candy.

Newport promised to return in twenty weeks, but he could spare only enough food from the ships' stores to feed the colonists for fifteen weeks. This meant everything at Jamestown had to be rationed from the beginning, as one hundred and five persons remained there. These included the parson, the surgeon, a blacksmith, a barber, a tailor, a drummerboy, six carpenters, a mason, and the conceited, overbearing man they had elected president.

Their wheat was coming up in the clearings, and they were quite hopeful of their prospects until the fierce damp heat of the long Tidewater summer began. Because these broad rivers emptied into the sea along this coast, the salt water came up into them with the high tide. When the tide went out again, the river water was still not as fresh as it should have been and sometimes was slimy and had an odor. However, the colonists used water from the river for their cooking and drinking, and this caused much sickness among them.

They were not used to the intense heat, which brought out many insects besides the mosquitoes which carried the fever. Their only food was half a pint of wheat and barley boiled with water for each man each day. The grain had already spent twenty-six weeks in the holds of the ships, and the settlers said it "contained as many worms as grains." They tried to raise a few chickens, but these didn't last long among so many appetites. There were no sheep or cattle, so they had no butter, milk, or meat. They caught some crabs and fish, and ate roasted squirrels and oysters, but were unable to get many deer or other large game. "Our drink was water and our lodging castles in the air," one of them wrote sadly, after Newport's ships had sailed. The public storehouse was often robbed, and people hoarded what little food they could hide, while their less fortunate or more honest neighbors went hungry.

Because they were sick and frightened, quarrels broke out among them, and their president was not strong enough or wise enough to control them and settle their differences. Most of all, they were homesick for the things they were used to in England and the comforts they had left behind. They wrote unhappily that there was no tavern or beer house where they could gather in the evenings as they did at home, and their only drink was the water from the river. Sick or well, each man had to take his turn at guard duty every three nights, whatever the weather.

By the end of September Captain Newport had been gone twelve weeks of his twenty, and there were fifty new graves, and men lay groaning in every corner of the fort. John Smith had proved to be the strongest and ablest man, and his friends started a feud with President Wingfield's friends. There was no discipline or authority. Under Smith's direction, and by his own example, he persuaded the few men who were well enough to crawl around to finish the building of the little houses they needed for shelter, and he himself was always willing to do most of the work. He also managed to trade with the Indians for corn and salted deer meat, and when the wild fowl flew south in the autumn some of them were shot down from the fort.

December came, and Newport had been gone six months. John Smith took a little open boat and half a dozen men and went up the river to find food. On the way they were attacked by Indians and two of his comrades were killed in the fight. He shot two Indians before he was overpowered and carried as a captive from one Indian village to another, where he was put on exhibition. He probably saved his life by showing the savages his compass, with its live, quivering needle protected from their fingers by glass. This seemed to them some kind of magic.

Finally he was brought to his friend the Powhatan's village, where the old chief received him in a long wigwam or communal house with a fireplace and benches. The chief sat on a sort of throne, on a rug of raccoon skins, "all with the tails on and hanging like ornamental tassels." He was surrounded by his young squaws, painted and ornamented with strings of white shells. Behind them stood the grim warriors of the tribe.

Although a friendship had already been established with these Indians, Smith had now killed two of the tribe and his life was to be forfeited. It is here that the romantic

John Smith was carried from one Indian village to the next, where he was put on exhibition

C S
Their
triumph about him
C. Smith bound to a tree to be shott to death
1607

story of Pocahontas began. She was at this time a child about ten or twelve years old. The familiar story goes that Smith was stretched on the ground with his head on a stone to have his skull crushed with tomahawks, when Pocahontas pleaded for his life, and then shielded his head with her own body until her father consented to spare his life.

Doubts have been cast on this story, but anyone can see that something must have happened to stop Smith's execution by a well-known Indian method. The Indian nature and custom would not have allowed the death of two Indians by Smith's hand to go unpunished. Years later when he wrote his own account of his adventures in Virginia, he told the story of Pocahontas as it happened. He apparently did not know that it was not unusual for an Indian spectator at a ceremony of torture or execution of a captive to claim him at the last minute as a brother, lover, son, or fellow warrior. It was not an act of pity, which the Indians did not understand, but a means to secure a useful addition to the tribe by adopting the victim as one of them. Thus, in return for his life they would gain his services and loyalty. This bargain would cancel out the blood debt as well as his death would have done. If Pocahontas had been older, he would probably have found himself bound to marry her, and perhaps this was thought of at the time. While she was still a child, high-spirited and playful, he was accepted by her tribe as her property and her friend. Her action therefore would not have surprised the onlookers as much as it did Smith himself. It was regarded simply as a whim of the chief's daughter, who would naturally be humored.

Smith's account tells how a few days later he was put through a formal tribal ceremony of adoption, and was then allowed to return to Jamestown, after promising to send back to the chief a grindstone and a small cannon. Pocahontas's childish friendship for the Jamestown settlement was proved more than once in the months to come. She made many visits to the fort, accompanied by a file of Indian attendants carrying gifts of venison, bread, and salted fish. An account written at that time says: "Very oft she came to our fort with what she could get for Captain Smith, that ever loved and used all the country well, and she so well requited it that when her father intended to have surprised him, she by stealth in the dark night came through the wild woods and told him of it. If he would, he might have married her."

But Smith regarded her as a child, perhaps to her own disappointment, and she behaved as a child, playing in the grassy streets among the cabins, running races and turning somersaults and "showing off" and learning to speak English from her indulgent friends. She was dressed in soft doeskin garments and moccasins, with a white feather in her dark hair to show that she was the daughter of a chief. Without the accident of Smith's rescue by Pocahontas and its lasting results of friendship, Jamestown might not have survived its first year.

Soon after Smith returned to the fort from this adventure, Newport finally arrived back from England. He brought food, equipment, instructions from the Company in London, news from home, and 120 recruits for the colony. This was known as the First Supply, in January of 1608.

Newport must have been astonished and saddened to find only 38 survivors of the 105 souls he had last seen at Jamestown. But the supplies he had brought were not enough for even the few survivors and the additional colonists who arrived with him. The colony was still far from self-supporting in the matter of food alone.

A dreadful fire broke out while Newport was still ashore. It consumed provisions, ammunition, shelters, and even part of the palisade. Sad, too, the Reverend Hunt's little library of precious books was burned to ashes, which would

Pocahontas begged her father, the Powhatan, to spare Smith's life

have been a great grief to him, but one of his companions recorded that "none ever heard him repine at his loss, and he was always as quick to answer an alarm and stand to defend the fort as any man there."

Newport set his sailors to help repair the damage, and went up the river with Smith where they made a deal with the Powhatan for more corn and dried meat. The chief renewed his promises of friendship. They carried to him presents from England—a sort of crown, a scarlet cloak, a basin and ewer somewhat like the ones the King used to wash his hands, and a bedstead. They had to explain to him the uses of these gifts—he would not bow his head to receive the crown, he was only used to seeing water carried in gourds, and Indians slept on piles of furs on the ground. The thing that pleased him most was a quantity of blue beads, which became a sign of Indian royalty and were reserved for the Powhatan's family only. In exchange, he promised to provide the settlers with food and to protect them with his friendship.

The fantastic hope of great wealth to be found in Virginia was the worst enemy the early settlers had. Newport's backers in London were demanding some return for their investment in the colony. He loaded his ship with cedar logs and some yellowish soil which they hoped would prove to contain gold, but which was without any value at all. "There was no talk, no hope, no work, but dig gold, wash gold, refine gold," Smith wrote in disgust, for he never had the gold fever himself. Newport also took home with him a pen full of twenty live turkeys, which he had got from the Indians by trading twenty swords.

President Wingfield returned to England with Newport on this voyage in April, 1608, and Smith must have been glad to see him go. In spite of Smith's courage and ability, the remaining colonists were still not ready to admit that he was the best man among them, and chose John Ratcliffe instead as their second president. The honor went at once to Ratcliffe's head. He insisted that a mansion house must be built for him suitable to his new importance, in place of the thatched shack he had been living in like everybody else. This useless work delayed the spring planting which should have been done for the sake of their food supply. The new arrivals all fell sick and had to be cared for by those who had become "seasoned" to the climate, water, and food.

Smith made another exploring trip northward during that summer of 1608. He went up the Chesapeake Bay into the Potomac and Susquehanna rivers, and proved once again that the hoped-for westward route to the Orient was everywhere blocked by land.

When he and his weary companions returned to the fort in September, they found that Ratcliffe had made himself so unpopular that he had been deposed. That is, he had been fired from the presidency, and his fine new house was left unfinished while more important work was done. The gentlemen-adventurers who had once looked down on Smith had learned their lesson at last. They invited him to take charge of the whole settlement, and gave him full authority to rule it.

chapter 3

The Starving Time

Smith was not the kind of man to hold grudges. He put everybody to work at whatever they could be taught to do. The soft palms of the "gentlemen's" hands were blistered by ax handles and saws, and they complained loudly about the hard labor they had never had to do before. Their curses caused Smith to make a humorous rule that every man who wasted his breath and energy swearing must have a can of cold water poured up his sleeve. This was uncomfortable in hot weather, and in cold weather it was a real hardship.

Working together at last, the settlers repaired the church, and built more cabins for the newcomers. A blockhouse was put up at the end of the little peninsula which connected Jamestown Island to the shore. This was a small square log building with holes left in its walls to shoot through, which they hoped would help to prevent unfriendly Indians from approaching the fort without being seen. Smith quite rightly never trusted the Indians' promises of peace and friendship, and kept an armed garrison at the blockhouse. The settlers also dug a deep well of "sweet water" inside the fort. This ended the use of the unhealthy river water for drinking and cooking.

In October, 1608, Newport was back again with the Second Supply. This time he brought seventy recruits, including two brave women—Mistress Forrest and her maid-servant, Ann Burroughs. There must have been a lot of sprucing up in that all-bachelor community when an unmarried woman arrived, and Ann was still in her teens. A carpenter named John Laydon won her hand in marriage. He had come out on the first voyage and had lived through all the hardships and perils since then. There was a church wedding, and they made the best feast they could to celebrate the occasion. The child born to Ann and John the following year was Jamestown's first baby. They named her Virginia.

A blockhouse like this one was put up at Jamestown

The passenger list of the Second Supply included some European artisans, or craftsmen—a few Poles and Dutchmen were encouraged to work at their trades. Soap and pitch were produced for the first time, and a furnace for making glass was set up. A few pieces of crude glass were actually made there for Newport to take back to England when he sailed in December, 1608. The ex-president Ratcliffe went with him, as well as a troublesome friend of his, the unpopular Gabriel Archer, which was a relief to John Smith.

In the midst of all the new industry, the usual care of their precious provisions in the storehouse was overlooked. Rats from the ships had come ashore and destroyed a large part of the grain and preserved supplies before they were discovered. This loss created a serious shortage of food for the coming winter. Smith sent some of the settlers to live at the oyster banks on the coast, to survive on the seafood they could find there—a diet which soon proved to be very unhealthy. Others went to the villages of friendly Indians who agreed to feed and house them. Pocahontas's friendship must have been valuable then.

There were fewer deaths during the second winter at Jamestown, thanks to Smith's hard authority. But by the summer of 1609 their reserve supplies had run very low and their new crops were not ready. The colonists who had been boarded out came back to rejoin the small group who had manned the fort all winter. The late arrivals were becoming "seasoned." Cold weather always reduced the fevers which were carried by the mosquitoes from the swamps which surrounded the island. No one would trace the infection to mosquitoes for another two hundred years, so they had no way to protect themselves from it.

Smith had sent a letter back to the Company in London by Newport's last voyage. In it he defended himself from the spiteful reports that he knew would be made by the discontented men who had sailed home with Newport. He begged the Company to send him more skilled labor in place of the dainty "gentlemen" who were unwilling to dirty their hands and had no idea of doing a day's work anyway. He told them he needed carpenters, blacksmiths, masons, gardeners, and fishermen. He also requested enough extra supplies to feed the new immigrants, so that he would not have to depend on the ships' crews to leave him whatever they thought they could spare.

This outspoken letter from Smith and the ill-natured accounts by men like Ratcliffe and Archer added to the dissatisfaction of the London investors. They were already disappointed in the results of their attempt to make fortunes in the New World. During the time that Newport was in England in the early part of 1609, a great change was made in the charters the Company had granted two years before when the Jamestown venture was started. Hereafter Jamestown would be ruled by a governor appointed by the Company, who was to live in the colony with the settlers. For this job they selected Thomas West, third Lord Delaware, whose younger brother Francis was already in Virginia. Also, the Company welcomed more investment in new shares by additional stockholders, who might be among the colonists themselves.

Many distinguished men and professional people like lawyers and clergymen took shares in the new corporation. Some of them sailed with Newport on his next voyage to see for themselves what it was like in Virginia.

People without an inheritance, or people out of work who were looking for a way to make money on a small investment, bought an interest in the colony and applied for passage, in order to take advantage of the single free share each settler was entitled to. This meant that he would be supported by the Company and live at their expense, while the proceeds of the colony's labor were thrown into a common fund, or pool, until a profit could be shown. As soon

NOVA BRITANNIA:

OFFERING MOST
Excellent fruites by Planting in
VIRGINIA.

Exciting all ſuch as be well affected
to further the ſame.

LONDON
Printed for SAMVEL MACHAM, and are to be ſold at
his Shop in Pauls Church-yard, at the
Signe of the Bul-head.
1609.

The title page of a 1609 emigration tract, which was used to attract new settlers to Virginia

as there was a profit everyone was entitled to an equal share in it, whether he had contributed much to the pool or little. To people who were ignorant of the conditions at Jamestown, this may have looked like an easy thing.

Some five hundred people, including women and children, assembled for the Third Supply. It required a fleet of nine ships to transport them and provisions enough to keep them for a while after they arrived in Virginia. In this new expedition the much-travelled Newport commanded a ship called the *Sea Venture.* Sir Thomas Gates sailed with him. Gates was a sturdy veteran of the European wars. Another passenger was Sir George Somers, an old admiral who was described as "a lion at sea and a lamb ashore." Gates was to act as Governor until Lord Delaware himself arrived with another fleet and more recruits. The Governor's appointment was for life, and it must have meant quite an upheaval for a man with property and relatives in the mother country. He needed time to make his arrangements to leave England, even though he would be able to return there on leave now and then.

Smith at Jamestown, of course, had not heard about all these changes, as there were no mails or communications except through busy Captain Newport, who shuttled back and forth across the Atlantic almost as though the passage was as easy as it is today. He was often many weeks at sea on the way.

The *Sea Venture* sailed from England with the Third Supply on June 1, 1609. On board other ships in the little fleet were Smith's old enemies Ratcliffe and Archer, who had spent the past months in England trying to discredit him.

The company had put all its best eggs in one basket, which was the *Sea Venture,* with Newport in command. Before the ships reached the coast of America late in July, they were "caught in the tail of a violent hurricane," which blew for two days and nights. The ships lost touch with each other, and one of them sank in the mountainous waves. The *Sea Venture* was blown so far off its course that it was wrecked on the rocky island of Bermuda, seven hundred miles from Jamestown. Most of its one hundred and fifty passengers and crew struggled ashore with what few belonging they could carry. The only living things they found on the land were herds of wild hogs left there by some former inhabitants who had disappeared. These animals provided them with food which probably saved their lives.

Newport, Gates, and Somers were men who knew how to take care of themselves and people in their charge. They began at once to build another ship from what was left of the *Sea Venture.* They salvaged her hardware and large timbers and added wood cut from the native cedars of Bermuda. It took them nearly a year to build two little boats. Their strange life on the beautiful, mysterious island was the basis for one of Shakespeare's most popular plays, called *The Tempest.*

Meanwhile, the other seven ships of Newport's fleet floundered on through the storm and finally came limping into the landing place at Jamestown. They brought some three hundred sick and exhausted passengers—the Third Supply. Children born during the terrible voyage had died. Fevers and disease from the close quarters on board had killed many adults, who had to be buried at sea. The stores of food brought for the use of the colony had spoiled in the heat or had been damaged by seawater during the storm.

A few live sheep and goats had survived the voyage in the battered, leaking ships. These relieved the worst needs of the settlers. But it was midsummer, and the arrival of many more disabled and helpless people just as the colony was beginning to pull itself together again under Smith's tireless leadership was hardly welcome to him. His distress and disappointment can be imagined when his old enemies

Ratcliffe and Archer came ashore among the passengers. They were triumphant with the news of the new charter, which appointed a governor over Smith's head. At the same time the storm had robbed him of the three men who might have supported him as the chosen leader of the colony.

The company's papers explaining the changes which had been made were all on the ship which had disappeared. Nevertheless Ratcliffe at once ordered Smith to resign in his favor. During the voyage Ratcliffe had collected a following of newcomers who were willing to be ruled by him. The old settlers knew Ratcliffe's faults and backed Smith, and so two rival parties were formed.

Smith refused to give up his authority until he had some proof of the company's wishes, or until the right people arrived. He continued to rule the colony just as he had been doing. Ratcliffe was so insulting to him, and caused so much bad feeling, that Smith finally had him arrested for disturbing the peace. This made for more ill will on both sides.

The settlers who were already living at Jamestown were mostly people of good character who had proved their courage. They had been through a lot together, and they gave Smith the credit for keeping them alive so long. Many of the newcomers were lazy misfits who were shocked and discouraged by the hardships they found awaiting them. Besides, the damp summer heat of the Tidewater soon affected their health.

Smith believed that the settlement should be moved to a better place than the low, marshy ground of Jamestown Island. He undertook to make a deal with the Indians farther up the James River for a tract of land in the hills near the present city of Richmond. The landscape there was so beautiful that he named the place Nonesuch. When he had bought the land and was on his way back to Jamestown, he was injured by an explosion of the gunpowder he carried in a bag in his little boat. He proved to be so badly burned that he could do almost nothing without better medical care than could be found in Virginia. He therefore decided to return to England on one of the Third Supply ships, which had been repaired and was ready to take some of the dissatisfied immigrants home again before the winter began.

It is possible that Ratcliffe and Archer made the most of this chance to force Smith to leave Jamestown, so that they could rule it without objections from him and his friends. In any case, he departed in October, 1609. He left about five hundred people at the settlement. Many of these were still new to Virginia. He took back with him a cage full of tame flying-squirrels, to amuse the King. These tiny creatures made charming pets.

Smith did not know he had been named by the Company in the second charter to work along with Gates. The new charter also praised him for his "care and diligence" in spite of what his enemies had said about him in London. But he never returned to Virginia. In 1615 he made a voyage to the Plymouth, Massachusetts, area, several years before the Pilgrim Fathers made their first settlement there. He spent the remainder of his life in England, writing his account of the Virginia colony and his adventures there. The map he made of that part of the New World was in use for generations. People returning from the colony to England often went to see him and were cordially received.

The ship which took him to England in the autumn of 1609 was the first to carry the news of the supposed loss of the *Sea Venture* and all on board, for nothing had been heard of the castaways on Bermuda. Governor Delaware departed at once for Jamestown, in April, 1610. He took with him about one hundred and fifty persons, and most of these were the skilled workmen Smith had been asking for. In Virginia, meanwhile, Ratcliffe and Archer could not agree on which of them should take Smith's place until the Governor arrived, so they chose George Percy to take command.

Percy was a younger son of the Earl of Northumberland. He had come out on the first voyage, as he had few prospects at home with half a dozen older brothers. Although he was still a young man, he was a veteran of the European wars and had managed to live through all the hard times at Jamestown. He could hardly have been called Smith's friend, but he had not openly tried to oust him from the command while he was there. Even Ratcliffe had to recognize Percy's rank and experience. After only three years of the damp climate and poor diet of the colony, Percy had aged rapidly and was in very poor health. He soon proved to be quite unable to exert himself to keep discipline and rule the colonists for their own good, as Smith had done. Ratcliffe was therefore allowed to do almost as he pleased. This was the worst possible thing for the people in his charge.

They ran short of food, with winter coming on. Ratcliffe set out with thirty of his followers to trade for corn and salted fish with the Powhatan up the river. But Ratcliffe had not Smith's way with the Indians. He angered them by his rude and threatening manner, and they killed him and all his party. His death left everything in Percy's hands again, and there was no leadership at all.

Conditions at the fort could hardly have been worse. There were not enough houses, and even then some of the older ones were torn down and used for firewood. In their desperation to keep warm, the colonists even stripped some of the logs from the palisade to throw on their fires. This left them at the mercy of the silent, deadly arrows of the Indians. After Smith's departure and Ratcliffe's blunder, the Indians became very unfriendly. Pocahontas was no longer seen in the streets of Jamestown. Her people watched with savage glee the sickness and death at the fort. Arrows flew

John Smith's own map of Virginia was used for generations

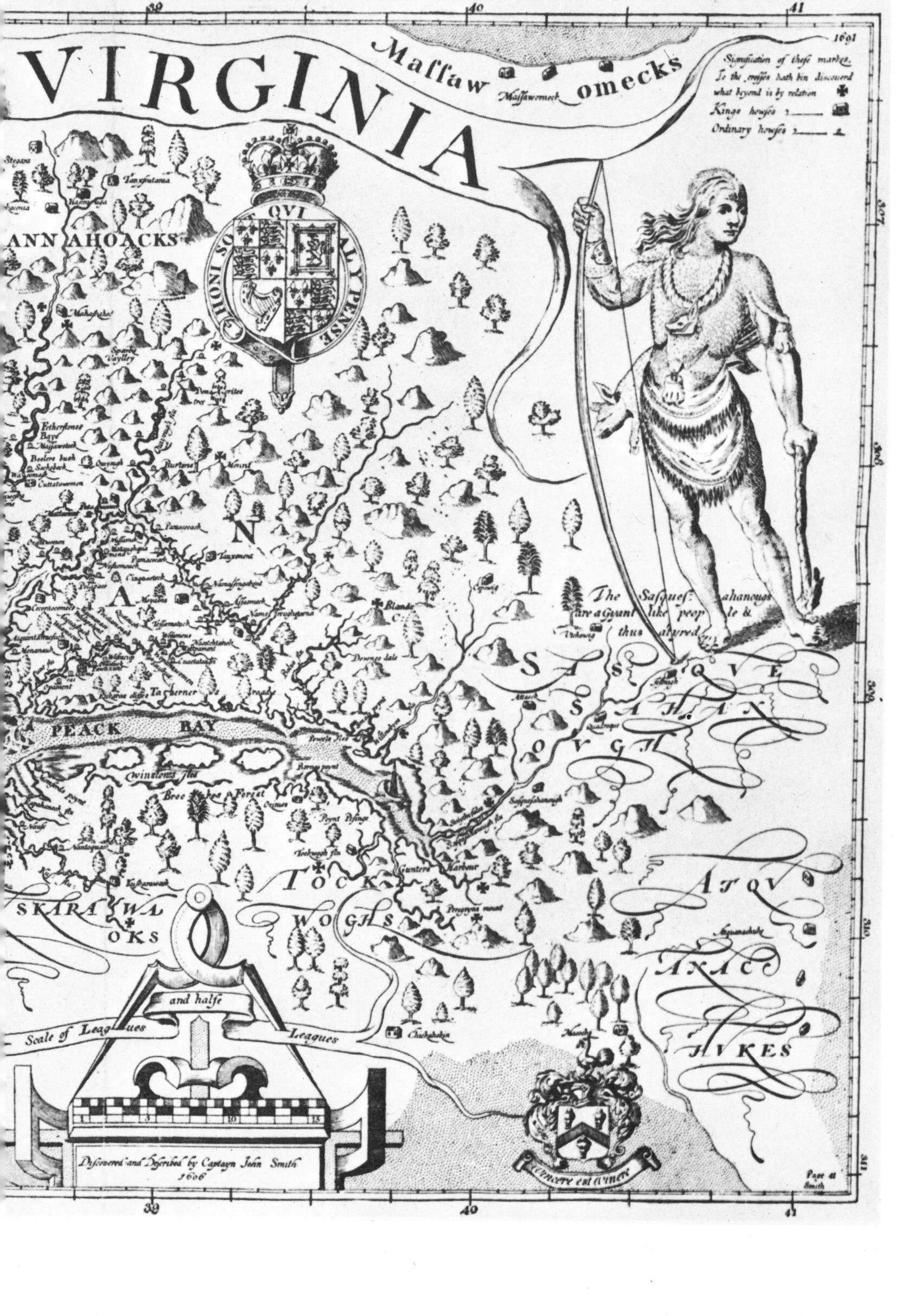
VIRGINIA
Maſſaw omecks
Signification of these markes.
To the croſſes hath bin discoverd what beyond is by relation
Kings howſes
Ordinary howſes
ANN AHOACKS
HONI SOIT QUI MALY PENSE
The Sasquesahanougs are a Gyant like people & thus atyred
PEACK BAY
SKARA WA OKS
TOCK WOGHS
and halfe
Scale of Leagues
Leagues
Discovered and Described by Captayn John Smith 1606
39
40
41

through the gaps in the palisade to kill people moving about the streets of the little village, and the fort was soon in a state of siege.

When the last of the stored grain and salted meat had been eaten, the starving population of Jamestown tried to find roots and herbs to live on. They ate every living thing that had flesh. They ate rats, mice, the last dogs and cats, even snakes. They finally turned to cannibalism, and cooked and ate the corpse of an Indian who had been shot at the palisade.

This was the terrible winter always to be known as the Starving Time. There was no leadership, no law and order, no decency, and no hope, at Jamestown. Some of the men tried to build a boat to go looking for food, and were drowned in it. Some of them ran away to beg for food from the Indians, and were murdered by them.

When spring came the five hundred people who had seen John Smith sail away had become less than one hundred bony wretches tottering around the tumbledown village inside the broken palisade. It could be said that if Smith had not had to leave Virginia he could have brought them through that winter in better shape, as he had done before. One of his friends wrote of his sorrow: "Thus we lost him who in all our proceedings made justice his first guide—ever hating baseness, sloth, pride, and indignity more than any dangers; who never allowed more for himself than for his soldiers with him; who upon no danger would send them where he would not lead them himself; who would never see us want what he either had or by any means could get for us; who would rather want than borrow, or starve than not pay; who loved action more than words, and hated falsehood and covetousness worse than death; whose adventures were our lives, and whose loss was our deaths."

A finer tribute than that, from one man to another, could hardly be found.

Meanwhile the tough, hardworking men at Bermuda were building the two small ships which they called the *Patience* and the *Deliverance*. They were eleven months at the job, while they lived on fish and the wild Bermuda hogs. They salted down and preserved both fish and pork as food for the voyage which they must still make to reach Jamestown. They actually managed to get there in May, 1610, and they found the half-crazed, haggard survivors of the Starving Time unable to believe that their friends from the *Sea Venture* were still alive.

Newport, Gates, and Somers listened with pity while the settlers pleaded to be taken back to England from a place which had become a horror to them, remembering the agonies and deaths of their companions. The three old-timers consulted together, and agreed that there was not enough food in their ships' stores to support the colony for long. They could see that the tragic remnant of Jamestown was in no shape to grow food and could never become self-supporting. They decided with regret that the attempt to colonize Virginia had failed and must be given up. They could do nothing else but offer to take the wretched Jamestown population on board their small crowded boats and sail up the coastline to Newfoundland. They knew that they could probably find fishing boats there which would take them back to England.

On a hot June day in 1610 the drums were beaten as though for a funeral. The colonists stripped the cabins of everything worth taking away and carried it aboard the *Patience* and the *Deliverance*. When the tide was right the two little boats set sail down the river, leaving Jamestown to the forest and the Indians.

But as the broad stream widened still more towards its mouth at Hampton Roads, they saw a longboat coming towards them. It was the kind of boat that merchant sailing vessels carried to take their passengers ashore, and it was rowed by English sailors. When it came alongside they learned that it had been sent ahead to announce the arrival of Governor Delaware's fleet. He was already at Point Comfort on his way in, with ships which were well stocked with fresh food and strong hands to re-establish the settlement.

It was that close. In another day or two he would have found the settlement deserted, as Roanoke had been. But Gates turned his little ships around and hurried back upstream. Weak as they were, and some of them in tears from exhaustion and excitement, the colonists tried to scrape up the miserable remains of their village into some kind of order before the Governor arrived.

When he stepped ashore on the bank outside the palisade, he found the gaunt, ragged population and the three stout captains from Bermuda and their passengers and crews all drawn up among the ruins to receive him in something like military style.

Jamestown was saved.

chapter 4

Lord Delaware Arrives in Time

Thomas West, third Lord Delaware and first Governor of Virginia, was another veteran of European wars. He was able to deal with disasters and downhearted followers, and he had a real talent for command. He was a fair man, and he was honest and kind.

He arrived at Jamestown to find what he must have thought was an appalling situation. He chose to take it all without blinking, and he made an impressive entrance to the fort, marching in with his colors flying, his drums beating, and his bodyguard lined up behind him in red cloaks and carrying spears. He was dressed in fine velvet and lace, which the tattered, unwashed colonists had not seen for a long time. He led the way to the church, where his chaplain delivered a solemn sermon. He made a speech to the settlers, warning them against idleness and despair, and urging them to new labors and courage for the sake of the colony.

Everyone took heart from his strength and courage.

Thomas West, third Lord Delaware, was the first Governor of Virginia

When they had had a few good meals from his supplies, they were ready to start rebuilding the fort and cabins with the help of the new tools and willing workmen he had brought with him. The church was repaired and dressed with a tall pulpit, a baptismal font, a walnut altar, and new cedarwood pews. The Governor was delighted with the beauty of the Virginia woods and wildflowers, and he required the church to be decorated with flowers and evergreen for all the services. He always attended in his best clothes, with his bodyguard around him, more for show than because he needed protection. A bell with a beautiful tone was hung, to call the people to worship or to work.

A young man named Thomas Dale had arrived with Governor Delaware. He was in command of the Governor's little army which came with him. The colony was still more afraid of starvation than it was afraid of the Indians. Delaware put Dale in charge of what was almost a military rule at Jamestown, which many people thought was too severe. Dale knew that they had been without any discipline or leadership so long that it was the only way to get things going again.

He went to work army style, and established some sanitation rules for the public health. He made the people clean their cabins and burn anything which might still be infected. He cleaned out the well, and would not allow them to use the river water for anything. He insisted on clean streets between the cabins, and new toilets were dug in the earth. Under his watchful eye things showed improvement at once, and the people could not help liking him, as they could see he was working for their good.

In September, 1610, Newport again sailed for England. Both Gates and Dale went with him, to report to the Company and urge it to send out more supplies and a better class of recruits. The winter of 1610–11 was not as bad as the Starving Time, but one hundred and fifty people died, and the Governor became very ill from the climate, the fever, and the food. Hoping that a little while in England would help him to recover, he left Virginia in March, 1611, and arrived in England that June after a long voyage. He named Percy to act as Governor for him until Gates and Dale could return and take command. Percy had already failed once to keep the colony in order, but there was no one any better. Delaware expected to find Dale and Gates still in England and promised to send them back at once.

However, Dale had already sailed with Newport for Virginia at about the same time Lord Delaware had left there. Gates was delayed in England on the Company's business, and appointed Dale as Marshal of Virginia, which gave him authority to run the colony alone until Gates could follow him.

This time Newport had three ships and about three hundred passengers, who were described as "a more shiftless and graceless set of ne'er-do-weels than had ever been sent out before." But Newport had loaded up enough food supplies to last the colony a year, and Dale turned out to be the best man Jamestown had seen since John Smith. He was a hardheaded soldier with a lot of common sense, and was compared to "an English mastiff," which was a large, savage hunting dog. But Dale was always a kind friend to those who behaved themselves, though he had little mercy for wilful wrongdoers.

Dale and Newport reached Jamestown in May, 1611, to find everything going downhill again under Percy's weak rule. Dale noticed with anger that men were playing at bowls in the streets during working hours, instead of cultivating the land and seeding for a new crop of food. He set up new laws approved by the Company, which provided severe punishments like whipping for a list of common crimes, and made it treason to speak ill of the King or the London Company. This discouraged grumbling, as treason meant a death sentence. No one was allowed to slaughter cattle or poultry for their own use without permission, or to trade privately with the Indians. The idle and discontented kind of people of course resented these new rules, and there was a plot to murder Dale. It was discovered in time, and the people who planned it were executed.

Dale was one of the first men to realize the true cause of the general failure of the colony so far. This was the compulsory system of throwing all the earnings and produce into a common stock which was then divided equally among them all, so that laziness was just as well rewarded as hard labor, and any one man's personal effort went for nothing so far as he and his family were concerned. Dale soon discovered that about one-fifth of the population was working hard to support the whole.

His common sense told him that to give a man a personal reason for working, like profit for himself and his family, by allowing him to keep the results of his own labor, was better than to drive him to plow and sow by flogging and brutality. With real courage of his own convictions, and with deep understanding of human nature, Dale took it upon himself to reform the communal system which the Company had imposed on the colony and which was not paying off. He changed the rules, so that instead of being treated like a machine, each settler was his own proprietor, with three acres of land for his own private use and benefit. For this privilege, he was required to pay a small portion of his produce into the public supply as a tax. Then if a man's family went hungry it was his own fault, and if he prospered he could keep his gains.

The effect was almost magical. People began to take pride in their own garden plots and cabins. Thrift became worthwhile, and each man tried to provide for his family as well or better than his neighbor did. Children were taught their father's skills, like blacksmithing or carpentry. A man's standing in the community depended on his own achievement compared to the next man's. Thefts from the storehouse and tale-bearing and little crimes and quarrels were less frequent, as each man began to mind his own business. And Jamestown never had starvation again.

Jamestown prospered under the strict rules of Thomas Dale

In August, 1611, Gates returned with six ships carrying two hundred men and twenty women, including his own wife and daughters. He also brought a good supply of cattle and provisions. In contrast to the jealous struggle for power which had plagued John Smith in the early days of the colony, Gates and Dale were old comrades and worked together in a friendly way for the best results. Gates was acting as Governor for Lord Delaware, who was still ill in England, and Dale was still the Marshal.

Together they revived John Smith's idea of finding a more healthful place to build a town than this riverside marsh, which could always serve as a landing place and outpost if the population moved farther up the river. In September Dale set out with three hundred and fifty men and laid out a place on seven acres of land on the north bank of the James, which he named Henrico for his friend, the eldest son of King James. The Indians had become more and more unfriendly since John Smith's day, as they realized the white men had come to stay and would occupy their favorite hunting grounds and clearings. Even Pocahontas's tribe had withdrawn in suspicion and resentment, and she had stopped coming to the fort.

At the new town of Henrico, a fort, a church, and storehouse were soon being built. There was a street of houses for families, and a building for the bachelors. The workers were often attacked by roving Indians, and some of the white men deserted to the Indian villages, perhaps in hopes of better food and Indian wives. If these runaways ever returned or were caught by the colonists, they were executed as deserters under Dale's strict laws, which were approved by Gates. Dale complained in his letters home that there were "many worthless and unruly people" in the settlement, and the Company at last began to improve the quality of the people it sent out to America.

Gates also changed the former policy of humoring the Indians in the hope of getting along with them. In his soldier's way he began to get tough with them and fought back, burning their crops and taking captives just the same as they did. The English wore armor plate, which turned the arrows, but their guns were clumsy and slow to fire.

There was a reckless young trader named Samuel Argall who owned his own boat and was always busy organizing fishing and hunting trips up the shoreline towards the Potomac, for the sake of more food. On one of these expeditions he came by accident on an Indian village where Pocahontas seemed to be paying a visit. Or she may have been married, at the early age of fifteen, to one of the tribe: the facts are not clear. Argall had never seen her before, but he had heard of her and knew her importance. He bribed her hosts with a copper kettle to help him coax her on board his boat, and then kidnapped her as a hostage for English prisoners taken by the Indians. She was doubtless willing enough to see Jamestown again, though her friend John Smith was no longer there. She said later that she did not know he had gone back to England.

She was cordially received at Jamestown, and found some old friends and made many new ones. Among the new ones was John Rolfe, who had sailed from England in the *Sea Venture* and was shipwrecked with Newport on Bermuda. During the months they spent on the island a child was born to Rolfe's wife and both the mother and child died. He had come to Jamestown on one of the two little boats they built at Bermuda, and saw the tragedy and despair into which everyone in Virginia had fallen. He had embarked with the survivors when Gates decided to try for Newfoundland, and was turned back with them when Delaware arrived at Point Comfort. Rolfe was the hardy, never-say-die type of man which Smith and Dale had always needed, and he set himself sensibly to make something of the new life he had chosen.

Rolfe smoked a pipe, and he missed his usual supply of tobacco when it ran out. He soon discovered that the Indians also had a kind of tobacco and used it in their tribal ceremonies and religious rites, and took comfort from smoking it in their several kinds of pipes. Tobacco had travelled to England by way of Spain about twenty years before, and Raleigh was one of the English who had adopted the habit. It was expensive, as the tobacco, the boxes to contain it, and the pipes all had to be imported from the West Indies or the northern coast of South America, where they grew a different kind of tobacco than that which Rolfe found in Virginia.

King James did not approve of the new fad, but many men dared to smoke anyhow, and insisted on its supposed benefits. A poet of the time wrote:

Earth ne'er did breed
Such a jovial weed,
Whereof to boast so proudly.

After nearly four hundred years, the argument over the use of tobacco is still going on, and it has now become much easier to get and much cheaper to buy in its various forms. The original Virginia tobacco which Rolfe found the Indians smoking was a coarse little plant with a yellow flower, and it bit the tongue. The West Indian plant had a pink flower and was much milder and sweeter scented. Rolfe sent for some West Indian seed and began to grow the pink-flowered plant in Virginia, where it flourished. It was a selfish plant, and sucked all the nourishment out of the soil, leaving it exhausted and unable to grow anything else. Rolfe bought enough land to raise a surplus crop beyond what was wanted in the colony, and he shipped it to England at a profit. This was the first export Virginia had been able to produce, and of course the Company was pleased.

When Pocahontas arrived in Jamestown as Argall's prisoner in 1612, young Rolfe was already having success with his tobacco growing, and was a respected and popular member of the colony. The Indian girl was turned over to the parson for instruction in the Christian faith, and in 1614 she was baptized in the Jamestown church and given the Christian name of Rebecca. She was then about eighteen, and Rolfe was thirty. We do not know the details of this famous romance. We can only imagine how it happened that in April of 1614 John Rolfe and the Powhatan's daughter were married in the church at Jamestown, with both Indians and English guests looking on in approval. A year later their son Thomas was born.

Like the diplomatic matches made between European thrones, this marriage was given credit for a long period of peace with the Indians. In 1616 Dale returned to England to look after his personal affairs there. Rolfe and his Indian wife and their baby son sailed in the same ship. When they got to London, Pocahontas, who always preferred that name to Rebecca, was presented at James I's Court by Governor Delaware's wife, and "carried herself like the daughter of a king." She was treated like a princess in rank, and was entertained at banquets and receptions and balls. She wore English dress, with the starched ruff and wide hooped skirts of the period. Her portrait was painted in this costume.

Naturally John Smith heard of her presence in England and came to call on her, greeting her as Lady Rebecca in the English style. This seemed to hurt her, and she turned away from him, covering her face with her hands. When he persuaded her to talk to him, she insisted on calling him Father, as she had always done when she was a child at

Indians and colonists gathered for the wedding of Pocahontas and John Rolfe

Pocahontas's portrait was painted in typical English dress

Jamestown. It was said that she had been told that Smith was dead, so that she would accept John Rolfe as her husband. She had always cherished her childhood devotion to the first white man she had ever seen, and might have preferred to marry him, in spite of the difference in their ages.

After they had been in England about a year Rolfe was appointed secretary to a new English Governor of Virginia, as Lord Delaware was too ill to return there. Rolfe made plans to sail at once for America, but Pocahontas fell ill at the last moment. It was probably pneumonia—from the cold English climate—and the disease was not understood then as it is now. She died before she could sail for home, and is buried in the churchyard at Gravesend, the seaport town where their ship was waiting. Her little son was left by his father with a relative in England and grew up there as an Englishman.

Rolfe returned to the colony with the new Governor and went on with his experiments in growing tobacco. The Virginia plant was now of a quality and taste which were as good as the original Spanish product, and could command a market in Europe. The colony had at last found something it could sell. Rolfe married again, in 1620, and set up a plantation on the north bank of the James River where he prospered.

Pocahontas's son Thomas came to America about 1640, when he was in his thirties, and married a Virginia girl named Jane Poythress. He had descendants which can still claim a drop of Indian blood, among them the Bollings and the Randolphs.

chapter 5

A Bride-Ship and a Massacre

By 1616 there was plenty of food in the colony, only six years after the terrible Starving Time. Livestock and poultry had been brought over in the later Supplies and had multiplied, and English seeds grew well in the Virginia soil. The population of the colony was still small—about three hundred and fifty, including several dozen women and children. The Indians were peaceful and the settlement had spread outside the Jamestown area on plantations and farms. There were soon six towns, which traded with each other and with the Company in England. Jamestown continued to be the center and the capital.

In 1619 the number of colonists was increased by eleven ships which brought over one thousand new immigrants and their provisions. Also in 1619 the first of the so-called bride-ships arrived, bringing ninety young women who had been selected by the Company as likely wives for the unmarried settlers who had begun to prosper and wanted to found families to inherit their hard-won property. The Company sent orders with these adventurous young women, to protect them as far as it could. They were to be placed at first with householders who already had wives, where they were to live until they were ready to make "good matches." They were not to be treated like servants, and they could not be forced to marry against their will. They were to be free to choose their own husbands.

How well these orders were carried out in that rough-and-ready society is a question. The girls certainly did not lack for a choice among suitors. Some of them caused trouble by becoming "engaged" to several men at a time, until a law was passed against such flirtatious behavior.

A false impression has grown up that the maidens were offered for sale by the Company to the settlers, like merchandise. The truth is that each bridegroom was required simply to repay the Company for the expenses of his lady's passage and keep during the voyage to Virginia. He paid this charge in tobacco, one hundred and fifty pounds of the best leaf per bride. It was also said that many of the girls were forcibly seized by the eager bachelors before they had more than set foot on shore. There may have been quite a scramble sometimes to escort the newcomers to their refuges in respectable married homes before they were claimed by men who were still total strangers to them. In any case, the first shipment of intended wives was such a success on both sides that others followed. A book called *To Have and To Hold* by Mary Johnston tells an imaginary story about one of the brides from the bride-ship.

Women continued to be fewer than men in the colony for years, but before long many pleasant homes had been set up to replace the rough cabins, with furniture brought out from England instead of the hand-hewn tables and chairs which had been the only comforts for so many lean years in the colony. Another ship brought more than one hundred boys and girls from the London streets. Probably many of them were orphans, and they were given this opportunity to begin as apprentices in the new trades which were growing up under the skilled workers described as "choice men, born and bred up to labor and industry," which the Company was at last providing. The vagabonds and worthless younger sons who had formed a part of the earlier passenger lists were no longer welcome. Many adults now came out to America as indentured servants. This meant they had bound themselves by contract to serve a certain master for a certain number of years just for their keep and lodging. After that they were to be given their freedom and a certain amount of provisions, so that they could begin a new life on their own. Many of them were ill-treated and the life they led while working out their time was sometimes little better than slavery.

In this same eventful year of 1619 there were important changes in the London Company and its government of the colony. A new charter commissioned the Governor to hold local elections for a General Assembly of representatives from each of eleven small communities called boroughs. There were to be two men from each borough, and they would be called Burgesses. This was the beginning of the Virginia Assembly. More than a hundred years later it would play an important part in the struggle of the Thirteen Colonies to free themselves from a tyrannical English Parliament and a German-born king. The Assembly met for the first time in the rebuilt wooden church at Jamestown on July 30, 1619.

It is interesting that in the same year that the colony got its Assembly and its brides, a Dutch trading ship arrived with a cargo of African Negroes to be sold as slaves. Possibly

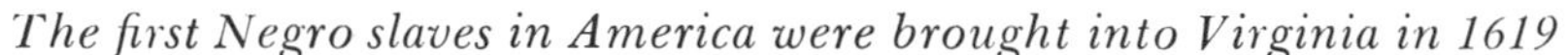

The first Negro slaves in America were brought into Virginia in 1619

they had been picked up in the West Indies, where they were already living as slaves. The cultivation of tobacco required hard labor, and always more and more land, as each crop wore out the land where it grew. The Negroes proved able to supply that kind of unskilled labor, but the growth of slavery was slow at first. The idea of slavery was not so hateful to the colonists as it is to us now, because in those harsh times, more than three hundred years ago, even captive white men and women were bought and sold in some parts of the world, such as Turkey and the Far East, and even among the American Indians.

The Governor's term of office was originally for life, but now it was changed to three years. In October, 1621, Sir Francis Wyatt arrived at Jamestown to preside over the local Council, which was a group of advisers to the Governor, and the Assembly. He was an upright, genial man of high birth—a man they could all look up to, unlike one of their own number raised up above them. He found a prosperous, busy colony, enjoying fairly good health and peaceful industry. It seemed as though the worst was over in Virginia. The colonists had set up ironworks, sawmills, and shipyards, besides their farms and tobacco plantations. More ships were arriving with better equipment and high-class labor. They had more cattle; they even had horses, for those who could afford them. They were preparing to manufacture such useful products as glass, tar, pitch, hemp, flax, pipe-staves, saltpeter, and even gunpowder.

Then on the morning of Good Friday, 1622, within six months of Wyatt's arrival, the Indians descended without warning on the outlying settlements and massacred more than three hundred and fifty of the colonists who had thought themselves safe among friendly natives.

The Powhatan had died in 1618 and his half-brother had followed him as chief of the tribe. His death at first seemed to cause no change in the relations between the tribes and the white men, who often opened their houses to the Indians as to each other. They gave them places at their dinner tables, and even a night's lodging. After eight years of peace, everyone went unarmed, and the Indians brought gifts of venison, turkeys, and furs, or offered to trade them for glass beads and other trinkets.

The Indians had planned the sudden attack so well that on the very day of the massacre many of them appeared as usual and sat down to a meal with their intended victims. Then as though at some signal they turned fiercely on their unsuspecting hosts and killed them with their own weapons, which lay openly within reach. They spared no one of any age or sex, and then savagely mangled the dead bodies. John Rolfe on his lonely plantation near Henrico was among the many valuable men who died that morning.

Jamestown itself was saved by the loyalty of an Indian boy named Chanco. He worked as the trusted servant of a settler named Pace on the south side of the James. Chanco had been ordered by his brother to kill his white master on Good Friday morning, but instead he warned Pace of the Indians' plans. Pace had just time to row three miles across the river and pass on the warning to the Governor in Jamestown. Because of Chanco's affection for his master, the town was not taken by surprise, and little damage was done there. The Indians always dreaded the white men's guns.

Terrified settlers who had not been in the path of the first attack began to pour into town with what belongings they could carry. Some of them even drove in their livestock as well. The refugees caused crowded conditions and a shortage of food at the fort. The massacre had come just at spring planting time, and prevented many farmers from getting their seed into the ground, so that a skimpy harvest

More than three hundred and fifty colonists were killed in the Good Friday Massacre of 1622

was feared. Food prices at once went up, until an order against profiteering was issued.

After the first shock of the massacre wore off, the colonists looked about them and found that there was less destruction than they had feared, although homesteads and food stores had been burned or stolen in a terrible waste. The London Company was not helpful. It seemed to think that the massacre was the colonists' fault for allowing themselves to be caught unready, and it advised a campaign of revenge. The colonists rallied to hunt down and kill the Indians who were known to have taken part in the treacherous attack, until they felt the score had been evened. The Indians were always more cunning than bold, and they fled into the forest and disappeared, so that an uneasy peace prevailed again.

After the colonists found courage to return to their deserted homes and make a new start, they still suffered from small raids and sudden murders at the outposts. Every house had to have a palisade around it, and a watch was kept every night, and workers in the fields carried their guns with them. They appealed to England for replacements of tools and supplies, and more ships arrived with donations of weapons and equipment, as well as new settlers.

But revenge is a bad basis for peace at such a price, and the old confidence and friendship between the white families and the once neighborly Indians were slow to revive.

During the summer following the massacre, many of the colonists died of a "plague" which seemed to arrive on the ship which brought out the Governor's wife to join him. Lady Wyatt was a brave woman. She had sailed for Virginia after the news of the Good Friday massacre had reached England, for she was determined to share her husband's daily life wherever his duty took him. She reported to her sister in a letter that the ship had been badly overcrowded, and many fell ill during the voyage. A number of new settlers, many of them invalids, had therefore arrived at Jamestown when the town was already full of refugees from the plantations, and food was running short. Conditions at the fort were favorable to the spread of any infectious disease, especially among the newcomers who were not yet "seasoned" to the climate. There were many deaths.

The Company now found that it had sunk what amounted to $500,000 in the colony, and the stockholders had received nothing in return. The new industries had not been successful. Tobacco was the only crop which paid, so it was being grown to the neglect of food crops for the storehouses. The Company criticized the colony, and the colony criticized the Company, until there was about as much ill-feeling in London as there had ever been in Jamestown. In 1624 King James dissolved the Company entirely, and made Virginia a Crown Colony, under his personal government. Hereafter he would appoint the Governor himself, and the Governor would report to him and not to a company. But he allowed the colony to keep its elected Assembly. Things were to continue like this until the Revolution in 1775.

Wyatt was the last Company Governor, and he was allowed by the King to continue in office for another year. He then returned home, and was followed by several unpopular royal appointments.

Under their rule, Jamestown outgrew its original boundaries and fortifications. Substantial houses were built outside the palisade on little plots of land with streets and gardens between them. The first brick house belonged to Richard Kemp, who was secretary to the colony. In 1639 the first brick church was begun, near the site of four earlier ones which had been built of wood and thatch. The first of these had been put up in 1607 inside the palisade, and was "a homely thing like a barn." It burned in the first fire at Jamestown the following year. The second church had been similar to it, and there Ann Burroughs was married to John Laydon in the colony's first wedding. Lord Delaware was responsible for the third church, larger and better furnished, where Pocahontas had been baptized and married. This one fell into disrepair, and a smaller one was built, where the first Assembly met. A fifth one was built outside of this, of buttressed brick with a tower. This church survives today as an ivy-clad ruin on the riverbank at Jamestown. Its walls are of handmade brick, and are three feet thick, and they have been standing for more than three hundred years. A Memorial Church adjoining it was built in 1907, for Jamestown's 300th birthday ceremonies, and it contains relics and memorials of the earlier buildings. In the churchyard only a few old stones remain to commemorate the countless dead who perished in the early days of the colony.

There were finally eighteen brick houses at Jamestown, "fair and large," which were occupied by the more prosperous families. March, 1641, saw the arrival of Sir William Berkeley as the Royal Governor. He became one of the most distinguished and powerful men in the colony for the next thirty-five years.

Shortly after Berkeley's appointment, King Charles I was beheaded by the Cromwellian government in England, and in the disturbances which followed the King's death, Governor Berkeley remained loyal to the Throne. He even offered refuge in Virginia to the cavaliers, or gentlemen, who were endangered by their support of the dead King or his heir, Prince Charles, who was in exile on the Continent. In 1651 the Commonwealth Parliament in England sent out a fleet to punish Berkeley for his loyalty to the monarchy, but he managed to make terms so that he could

This ivy-clad church at Jamestown has been standing for more than three hundred years

resign his post as Governor and retire to his own plantation called Green Spring, which was on the mainland just above Jamestown Island.

For a few years the Virginia Assembly was allowed to elect governors who acknowledged the authority of Oliver Cromwell, but Virginia's population was mostly Royalist in feeling. When the Restoration brought Charles II to the throne in 1660, the Virginia Assembly invited Lord Berkeley back as their Governor, with the King's approval.

Under Berkeley's firm Church of England rule, both Puritans and Catholics who arrived at Jamestown were

Charles II (left) restored Lord Berkeley (right) as Governor of Virginia

made so unwelcome there that they soon left for the New England and Maryland settlements, and so Virginia remained largely Episcopalian.

As time went on and he grew older, Berkeley became tyrannical and unpopular, and very hard to get along with. A series of disasters brought distress to the plantations which were spreading up the rivers. A year of violent storms and floods damaged the crops. England's war with the Dutch brought out Dutch privateers, or pirates, and strangled trade. There was a cattle plague. Worst of all, the Indians began to press inward again on the western frontier, as the growing New England settlements crowded them out of lands they had always considered their own. They therefore wanted to reclaim land the Jamestown settlers were moving into.

Governor Berkeley seemed to be doing nothing to encourage or support the people who depended on him. They paid a tax for protection from the Indians, but the raids on lonely homesteads on the western and northern borders of the colony went unpunished. Instead of sending out an armed force to drive the Indians back, the Governor made vague plans for new forts which were never built. He had gathered around him a group of wealthy and do-nothing cronies who now made up the Assembly. He managed to put off the usual annual elections of new members year after year, so that all power remained in his hands. He married a young wife when he was in his sixties, and while she defended his bad temper and bullying ways, she did not improve his disposition.

The plantations now extended up the banks of the James River as far as the present site of Richmond. Across the peninsula beyond Jamestown the Middle Plantation had grown up, where Williamsburg now stands. The people in the exposed locations were ready and willing to form their own army of volunteers to drive off the Indians, but they lacked the leader which it was the Governor's duty to supply. About 1676 a young man named Nathaniel Bacon put himself at their head without consulting Berkeley. His fiery speeches and brave example attracted a loyal following who demanded the right to act as an official commissioned army against the Indians.

Berkeley distrusted any armed force which opposed his own failure to act, and refused to give Bacon a commission to lead it. Bacon was a recent arrival in the colony, who had established himself at a place on the James called the Curles, where the river made loops and created islands and backwaters in a rich and picturesque scene below the falls where Richmond now stands. His young wife had come out to join him, and he feared for her in such an exposed spot. He swore that "commission or no commission, if the redskins meddle with me I'll harry them!" At a time when the Bacons were fortunately absent from their home, the Indians raided Curles and killed Bacon's overseer, who was also his friend. Some damage was done to the house and the crops, and the savages disappeared again into the forest.

Bacon was furious, and his friends gathered around him. He led this little force to Jamestown, planted them in front of the State House, where the Governor and his cronies were in session, and loudly demanded a commission to lead an army against the Indians. In a theatrical scene, like something out of a play, the Governor appeared in the doorway and dared Bacon to shoot him down. Cooler heads interfered, and the Governor promised the commission.

Bacon accepted his word for the deed, and led his men into a skirmish with the Indians on the south bank of the James, which he won. The Governor then took fright again, and roared that Bacon had acted without a commission and that they were all rebels. After some discussion, he yielded to public opinion enough to call a new election, the first in fourteen years. Bacon's Henrico neighbors chose him to represent them, and he arrived at Jamestown with forty armed followers to take his seat in the Assembly.

Again there was an argument and even some shots were fired. Bacon was finally persuaded to appear before the Governor in the Council chamber and make an apology for having acted without a commission and defeated the Indians. It looked as though the difficulties had been ironed out and the commission would finally be granted. But that night while Bacon lodged with a friend in the town, he received a warning that there was a plan to seize and imprison him. He left his wife in his friend's protection and fled in time to his property at Curles, and there his supporters rallied around him.

Once more in this seesaw tragedy of errors and mistrust, he could be made to look like a fugitive and a rebel against the Governor's authority. Berkeley told Bacon's wife that he would hang her husband when he caught him, and tried

Nathaniel Bacon demanded of Governor Berkeley a commission to lead an army against the Indians

to gather together an army to go and hunt him down. Berkeley was by now more afraid of Bacon as a threat to his own personal power than he was of the Indians. But very few men were willing to support the Governor against a man they sympathized with, and he left Jamestown for a camp in Accomac, across the water from where Yorktown now stands.

The Indians took advantage of the confusion and quarrels among the English to murder and rob in the countryside on the Pamunkey River above Jamestown. They killed four or five people at a time, wherever they came across them, and burned crops and homesteads. Bacon took revenge for the murders in the Pamunkey country, and set up his headquarters in the Governor's mansion at Green Spring. As Jamestown had been deserted by the Governor, Bacon went in and burned the town, with the aid and consent of his friends who lived there. Some of these went so far as to set fire to their own homes, including the finest brick houses in the colony, just to prevent the Governor from using the town as a base for his campaign against Bacon.

So far Bacon had had the wholehearted support of a large number of the colonists, but now he made a mistake. He knew that he had gone so far that failure would mean his death on the scaffold for treason. He did not realize that the discontent of the people who had joined him was with the Governor himself and not with the King. So when he heard a rumor that the Governor had sent to England for a regiment of troops to back him, Bacon asked his friends for an oath that they would help him to resist the King's soldiers if they came. This would have been a hanging matter for everybody concerned, and many of the men surrounding him drew back. While he was in camp at the Middle Plantation near Green Spring, planning an attack on the Governor's forces, Bacon was overtaken by a

Bacon and his followers burned Jamestown

fever and sickness as a result of his exertions in the hot, damp summer weather, and died at the age of twenty-nine.

It is easy to compare the Bacon Rebellion of 1676 to the Revolution of 1776, but the comparison has weaknesses.

Bacon led a protest against the willful bad government of an ill-tempered Governor, and taxation which brought nothing in return. But his desperate resolve to fight the King's troops if they were sent to restore order was too soon by almost a hundred years, and it rose out of Berkeley's mistakes and was not a quarrel with the King or the British Parliament, as happened later. The little war lasted only a summer, and Bacon's death meant its speedy end, as his execution would have done if he had lived long enough to fail.

He has been glorified as being a man ahead of his time, and he has been belittled as a hotheaded youth playing soldiers with his life as the stake. It is safe to say that he was neither. He was no Cromwell, and did not wish to rule in Berkeley's place. He did not go off half-cocked to free all Virginia from Royal injustice. He was a young man, reckless, brave, and loyal to his friends, and he believed he was taking their part against the elderly, soft-living Governor and his shortsighted companions. Bacon feared also for his young wife's safety and the future they meant to make for themselves in this dangerous new world of Virginia. He had everything to lose, and he risked it gallantly, until there was no turning back. Like so many rebellions against the established order of things, his had to fail. But not altogether. It was needed, it was done, and at its price it did accomplish something. Governor Berkeley was recalled to England by the King to give an account of what had happened.

Charles II had seen his father's reign end in violence and murder. He had felt his own life in danger more than once. He was pleasure-loving and witty and liked his pretty ladies, but he had lived hard in exile and his indifference was often a pose to hide a very keen intelligence. He did send a regiment of red-coated soldiers to restore order in his colony of Virginia. He sent with them three worthy and fair-minded men who were decently horrified at the revenge Berkeley had taken on the little band of men who had defied him. It did not matter to Berkeley that the so-called rebels had at last succeeded in scaring off the Indians by the only method the savages understood—they had killed a great many Indians in return for the lives of more than three hundred settlers who had died by torture, treachery, and murder in their homes.

Berkeley had not waited for the King's representatives to arrive. All through January, 1677, the trials and executions went on at Green Spring. He had the house repaired and refurnished after its occupation by Bacon's force, and he simply seized from other houses the furniture and livestock he wanted for his own place. Bacon's friend Drummond, who had fired his own residence that night at Jamestown, was hanged the same day he was caught, though it left his widow penniless and on the charity of her husband's friends. Another man's wife made a dramatic appeal on her knees to the Governor, blaming herself for her husband's presence in Bacon's ranks—but he was allowed to die in prison. A few of Bacon's friends escaped into the swamps in winter weather and were never heard of again. Before the King's shipful of soldiers could arrive at the fire-blackened ruins of Jamestown, there had been more than twenty executions—Berkeley took more lives, the King said, than he himself had required to atone for the death of his father on the scaffold in 1649.

When Berkeley sailed for England, he left his wife at Green Spring, probably to show that he meant to return as Governor. He died soon after reaching England, and she married again, one of his friends named Ludwell. But she thought so highly of her title and position as the Governor's wife that her tombstone in the Jamestown churchyard carries her name as *Lady Berkeley*.

chapter 6

The Middle Plantation Becomes Williamsburg

The King had named one of his three commissioners to stay on in Virginia as Governor until a new man could be sent out. During the next twenty years several Royal Governors came to Virginia. Some of them were good. Some of them were bad. Charles II died and his brother James came to the throne. James died and his sister Mary and her husband became King and Queen. She had married a man called William of Orange in the Netherlands, and he would be known as William III of England.

The colonists rebuilt Jamestown after the fire there. They built a new State House, where the elected Burgesses met to make the local laws. They also built more solid brick houses. The Indians were quiet until the summer of 1681. Then the tribe called Seneca terrified the settlers in the Potomac country north of Jamestown. The settlers in Maryland were troubled by disease and poverty. On the other side of Virginia, North Carolina gave refuge to runaway servants and criminals, until it was sometimes called "the sink of America."

But for years the Virginia colony suffered from mismanagement and became so hard up that the colonists cut down their tobacco plants because too much tobacco was being produced for the market. This had brought the price of tobacco so low that nobody could make any money out of it. Finally things became so bad it looked as though there might be another rebellion like Bacon's. They wanted a new Governor. In 1690 William III sent out Sir Francis Nicholson to govern the Virginia colony.

Nicholson knew about America, as he had already served in Maryland and New York. He was not married, and lived in a small rented house in Jamestown. When he did not have guests for dinner, he went to a nearby tavern to eat his meals. This was a very simple way for a Governor to live. He had a quick temper, and was soon famous for his rages.

King William III

Queen Mary

First of all, he made a tour of the border defenses against the Indians, to see how the people were doing who had built forts and palisades to protect their homes. After he came back from the border, he began to pay attention to the civil laws in the older part of the colony, to encourage the people to manufacture what they could and to trade with other colonies and abroad. He started a free school, and proposed a college where the native Virginians could learn to be lawyers and parsons and schoolmasters.

A Scottish clergyman named James Blair held the highest office in the church, as the colonies did not have a bishop until after the Revolution. Blair was called the Commissary, and was entitled to a seat in the Council and a voice in the laws. He was so well thought of in England that the Virginia Assembly voted to send him to London to ask the King and Queen for a charter, or license, to start a college in Virginia. He raised quite a sum of money towards its cost, and got more money in England, along with the charter. He was named president of the college by the King and Queen, and held that position for more than fifty years.

Soon after he returned from England in 1691 the foundation of the college was laid at the Middle Plantation, which was on a ridge of land between the James and the York rivers, After the Indian massacre of 1622, the settlers had built a palisade across this neck of land above the Middle Plantation, to keep the Indians north of it and let the settlers build south of it. There were already a church and a little village there, when they founded the college.

The plans for the college buildings were said to be drawn by Sir Christopher Wren, who was a famous architect in England at that time. It is the only building in America which has the honor to be built from his plans. Their first building burned down after a few years, but they rebuilt it again the same way. The old bricks of that building are still standing at the College of William and Mary. The only college in America which is older is Harvard, in Massachusetts. It was founded in 1636.

The first teachers at the College of William and Mary were the President, a grammar master, a writing master, and a professor of mathematics. There was also a man called an usher, who was a sort of assistant teacher and did all the errands. By the middle of the 1700's, they added a department of medicine and a department of law.

The Phi Beta Kappa Society began here in 1776. It was a secret club, and the first college fraternity. Its name came from a Greek motto which said: *Philosophy is the guide of life.* New chapters of this society were founded at other colleges later on as they came to be built. The membership of the Phi Beta Kappa Society was limited to students of the highest degree of learning, and still is. At first no women were elected to it. There were no women at the College of William and Mary either until 1918.

The College was built at the western end of the long, wide street which runs down the middle of the town of Williamsburg, which grew up around it. At the College gate the road divides, and one way goes to Richmond and the other leads to Jamestown. There is a pretty green triangle of lawn with old trees around the College buildings.

The square brick building on the left of the gate is called Brafferton. It was the first Indian school in the colonies which lasted any length of time. It was opened in 1723, endowed by a rich man who gave the money to start it. The square brick building which faces Brafferton from the other side of the gate is the President's House. It has been occupied by all twenty of the Presidents of the College, including the first one, President Blair.

The only known drawing of the first college building at William and Mary

The President's House was claimed by the British General Charles Cornwallis as his headquarters when he was at Williamsburg during the Revolution. This was in 1781, just before he was defeated by General Washington at Yorktown. The main building of the College was used as a hospital by the French troops who had been sent over to help Washington win the war. All the College buildings have suffered from fires, but have always been rebuilt. The Rockefeller Restoration program has now restored the whole town of Williamsburg so that it looks the way it did in the 1700's.

The first commencement exercises were held at William and Mary in 1700. Both Indians and Virginians were present. Other guests came from as far away as Maryland and Pennsylvania.

The early teachers, who were called the faculty, kept records of their meetings. These are interesting to a modern student, as they show how the boys who went to William and Mary lived. There was a matron, or housekeeper, who was supposed to look after their laundry and their food. She was also supposed to see that they got their medicine when they were sick. Either pies or pudding had to be served to them twice a week, to be sure they got their dessert. She was not allowed to make up their suppers out of scraps from the midday meal, though she could hash up cold meat for them. A stocking-mender was hired to live near the College—everybody wore knee-breeches then. No scholar was allowed to keep a race horse in the town, or to bet on the races. They were also forbidden cockfighting, cards, and dice. They were not to go into the taverns, which were called "ordinaries," where liquor was served. These rules were so plainly posted that nobody could pretend to be ignorant of them.

All the professors or teachers were bachelors and lived at the College. One of them, Parson Camm, tried to help a friend of his who wanted to marry a girl named Betsy Hansford, and wasn't making much progress in his courtship. As he was a preacher, Camm quoted Bible texts to the girl, choosing those which urged marriage as a part of everyone's duty. Betsy listened to him very patiently, until one day she gave him a Bible text herself—II Samuel xii.7. Camm had to look it up. Imagine his surprise when he found: "*And Nathan said to David, Thou art the man!*" This made it pretty plain that she would rather marry Parson Camm than his friend. He took the hint, and they were married. After that the College passed a rule that if a professor married he had to give up his post.

Early in 1699 there was another fire at Jamestown. This time it was only an accident, but the State House where the Assembly met was damaged, and when the Burgesses met in April, they soon moved to the still unfinished buildings of the College at what was still called the Middle Plantation. At that meeting they decided to leave Jamestown forever, and make the village near the College the seat of the government. They named it Williamsburg, and set aside a piece of land at the other end of the main street on which to build a new State House. This came to be called the Capitol, and was a handsome building made of brick, with rooms for the Assembly and the Council to meet in. They brought out fine oak furniture from England for it, and it was as handsome a building as could be found in all the colonies.

Governor Nicholson was very much interested in the new town, and himself drew up a plan for its streets. He designed the streets to form a cypher, or monogram, of W and M, for King William and Queen Mary, but this had to be given up as the land was not flat enough. They named the central street for the Duke of Gloucester, Queen Anne's son, and gave names like Francis and Nicholson and King and Queen to the side streets.

It was a much healthier place to live in than Jamestown, as it stood on higher land between the York River and the James, and there were creeks on either side for small boats

Governor Spotswood spent so much money on the new Capitol Building (below) that people called it the Governor's Palace

to use. Most of the travel was still by water, as the roads were so bad. Fairs and markets were established, and people said that the Middle Plantation with its new name of Williamsburg grew more in six years than it had in the past sixty. By the time the Revolution started in 1775, Williamsburg compared in importance, though never in size, to Philadelphia and Boston.

Sir Francis Nicholson was on the whole a good governor, except for his violent temper. Complaints against him were sent to England, and he was recalled in 1710.

Governor Alexander Spotswood arrived in Williamsburg the same year. People liked him. He found the new Capitol Building finished and in use, but the house they were building for the Governor to live in was not yet ready. It stood midway of the main street, with a large green lawn in front of it. Governor Spotswood took pleasure in finishing it for himself, and he spent so much money on it and made it so grand that people called it the Governor's Palace.

William and Mary had no children, and Mary's sister Anne had become Queen after William's death, in 1702. The Virginia colony was prosperous now, and people had money and nice homes and could provide themselves with the comforts and luxuries they had left behind in England. The owners of the big plantations shipped their tobacco to England and applied the money in their accounts there to buying fine furniture and silks and velvets, as well as the necessary household goods, china and silver, and preserved foods like raisins and spices and sugar, and medicines. They even built a theater at Williamsburg, and companies of actors came out from England to perform plays by Shakespeare, Beaumont and Fletcher, and by other dramatists who are now almost forgotten. They had a racetrack. They started a postal system, with men on horseback riding from

Philadelphia to Williamsburg and back every two weeks, to carry the mail. One of the first newspapers in the colony was printed at Williamsburg. They called it the *Virginia Gazette*. Its owner erected the first paper mill in Virginia, on the outskirts of the town.

In 1722, just one hundred years after the terrible Indian massacre of 1622, there were one thousand people and more than two hundred houses at Williamsburg. When the Assembly met at "the public times" in the spring and autumn, the town was crowded with the Burgesses and their families. Brightly painted coaches rolled through the sandy streets, attended by the men of the family riding well-groomed saddle horses. Every day there were balls and banquets and lawn-parties and fairs, with fireworks in the evenings.

Not all of the Burgesses owned houses in town besides the elegant brick mansions they were building on their plantations, which lay along the banks of the great tidal rivers. Tidal rivers flow into the sea, and when the tide is high salt water rises up into the fresh for miles above their mouths. Quite large ships could come right into the landings which were built along the banks below the houses. Great mansions like William Byrd's Westover and the Harrison family's Berkeley all faced the river instead of towards the little muddy roads behind, because their guests arrived by water in their own barges, which were large open boats rowed by servants in livery.

Inns and taverns were built in Williamsburg so that the Burgesses and their families would have a place to stay and to entertain their friends during the gay Assembly times. The most famous of these was the Raleigh Tavern, which stood halfway along the main street in a yard with a bowling-green behind. It had a fine supper room, with a crystal

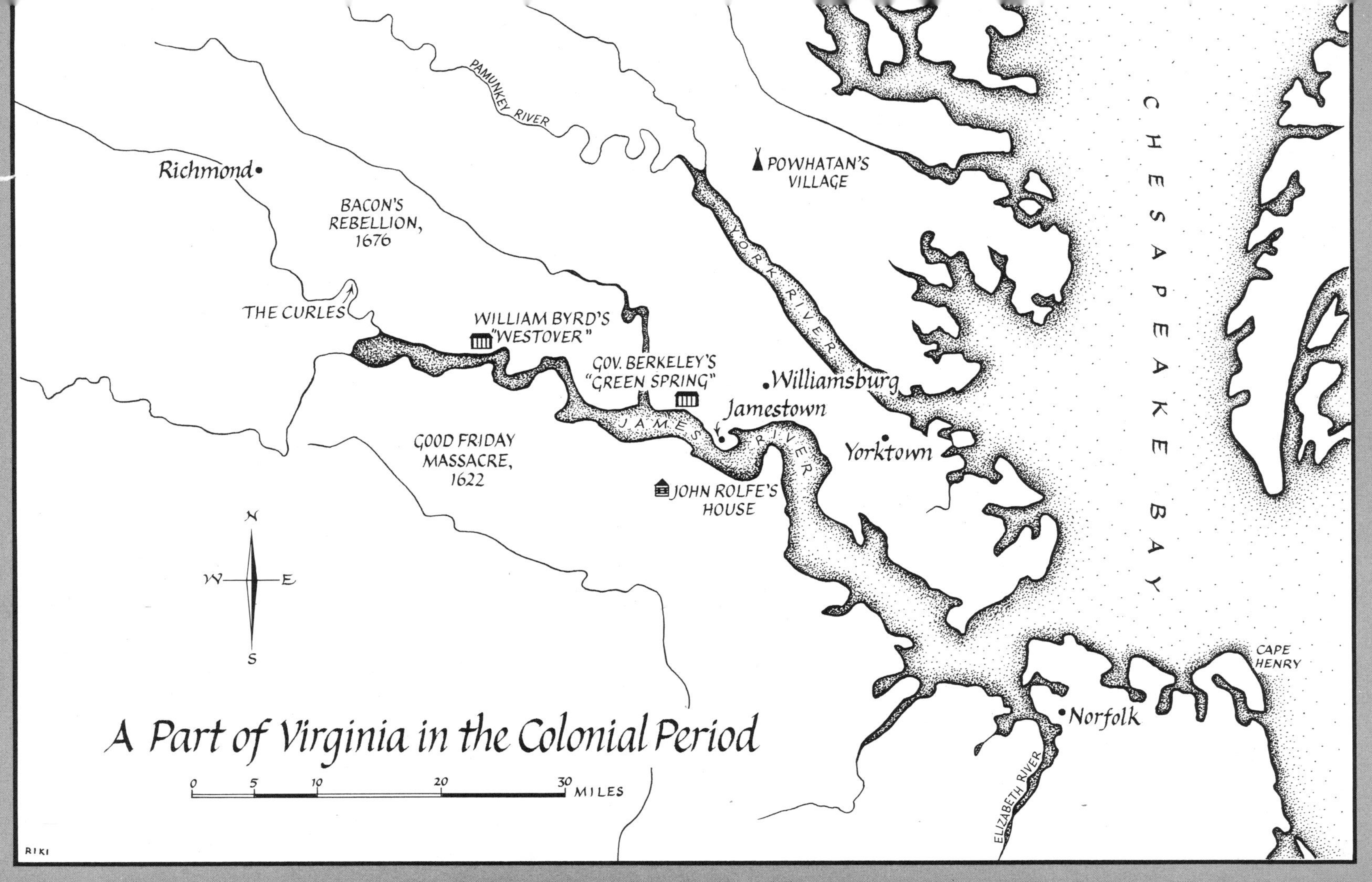

CHESAPEAKE BAY
PAMUNKEY RIVER
Richmond
POWHATAN'S VILLAGE
BACON'S REBELLION, 1676
YORK RIVER
THE CURLES
WILLIAM BYRD'S "WESTOVER"
GOV. BERKELEY'S "GREEN SPRING"
Williamsburg
Jamestown
JAMES RIVER
Yorktown
GOOD FRIDAY MASSACRE, 1622
JOHN ROLFE'S HOUSE
N
W
E
S
CAPE HENRY
Norfolk
ELIZABETH RIVER
A Part of Virginia in the Colonial Period
0
5
10
20
30
MILES
RIKI

chandelier, where club meetings, political debates, and private parties were held.

Queen Anne survived all her heirs, and her death in 1714 was the end of the Stuart royal line in England when George I succeeded her. His claim to the British throne rested on a rather distant relationship to Anne. His father was a German prince and his mother was a granddaughter of James I. He had been born and brought up in the German state of Hanover, in the Protestant faith as England's law required its rulers to be. That is how it happened that after Anne's death the throne of England came to a German prince, who did not speak English and had no understanding of the tradition of personal rights and freedoms which had been guaranteed to the English people by their Magna Charta as far back as 1215. Most of the Continental rulers in George I's time were despots—men with unlimited personal power. The first Hanoverian kings who came to England were a stubborn, narrow-minded, strong-willed family, used to having their own royal way about everything. England did not very much like its new German monarch, but it put up with him, and three more German Georges were to follow the first. It was the third one who collided head-on with the young, free-thinking colonies across the Atlantic and lost them forever as a British possession.

The next great Governor to arrive at Williamsburg was William Gooch, in 1727, the year that George II followed his father as King of England. Gooch was to have the longest term of office so far—twenty-two years—during the greatest prosperity the colony had ever known. He was said to possess "the happy faculty to balance the Assembly on one hand against the lords of trade upon the other, and to smile with amiableness upon the people besides." Under his wise guidance the laws that controlled the trade in tobacco were

Governor Dinwiddie

improved, to the advantage of the planters. So the record reads: "Whereas Spotswood had built prosperity, Gooch built yet greater prosperity upon it."

The westward settlements were extended, and the great plantation houses increased in number and grandeur at this time. Gooch himself was impressed by the elegance and style of the colony he had found flourishing on the edge of the wilderness, and wrote his brother in England that "the gentlemen and ladies here are perfectly well-bred, and not an ill [bad] dancer in my government." By dancing he meant the formal minuets and quadrilles which were performed in the Palace ballroom to the music of violins and a harpsichord, which was a kind of early piano.

Gooch resigned in 1751 because of bad health, and Robert Dinwiddie, who took his place, was soon installed with his family in the Palace. It was during his time that the French and Indian War took place, and a young soldier named George Washington was first heard of.

chapter 7

The Frontier Moves Westward

In the middle 1700's the western boundary of Virginia had still not been explored or mapped. For more than a hundred years it had been supposed to include land which we now think of as Pennsylvania, extending even as far west as Illinois and Wisconsin. But the French were coming down from their Canadian settlements and taking over the still unoccupied land in the fertile valleys along the Ohio and the Monogahela rivers. Governor Dinwiddie of Virginia said that all that land belonged to Virginia, and sent out a young surveyor to warn the French not to trespass. His name was George Washington.

He returned to Williamsburg to report that the French would not give way. Two years later, in 1754, Dinwiddie gave Washington the rank of lieutenant-colonel—he was twenty-two years old—and sent volunteer militia with him to force the French out of the Ohio land west of Pittsburgh,

George Washington as a young surveyor

which was then only a fort the French had named Duquesne in the forest. There Washington fought his first battle, at a place called Great Meadows, where he had built a hasty palisade fort which he called Fort Necessity. His men were much weakened by disease and casualties, and after a sharp skirmish he had to admit defeat and withdraw.

It was no discredit to him, although when he returned to report to the Governor, Dinwiddie would not accept the French claim to victory. George II backed up the Virginia claim to the western lands by sending out Royal troops under General Braddock—the famous British "redcoats." From this conflict in a wilderness which we call the French and Indian War the quarrel spread to the old European rivalry between France and England, and became the Seven Years War, which was fought on two continents and finally involved most of the countries of Europe.

George Washington knew the frontier country firsthand from boyhood and had already dealt with the tricky Indians, so he was assigned to accompany Braddock on the Monongahela campaign as a member of his Staff. The French had hired and bribed the Indians to fight on their side. Braddock did not understand wilderness warfare and would not listen to advice from those who did. He insisted on fighting European style, with his men in column, firing at command and marching elbow to elbow in their bright red coats. On the long march to the Ohio his army was caught in ambush and forced to fight a battle near where Pittsburgh is today. The French and Indians fired on the British from behind rocks and trees and slaughtered the red-coated men who could not even see where the bullets were coming from. Braddock was defeated and died on the battlefield.

George Washington was the only man on Braddock's Staff of officers who escaped being wounded or killed that day, though he was in the thick of the fight, and had three horses killed under him, and several bullets passed through his clothes without hurting him. It was said later that he seemed to have a charmed life, to preserve him for the great destiny ahead of him.

Having distinguished himself for bravery under fire, young Washington found himself famous when he returned to Williamsburg to tell the Governor about the battle. Braddock's defeat left the Indians free to terrorize the frontier again, so that no isolated family, even in the Winchester area, could feel safe. For a while the westward flow of settlers stopped, and the pioneers fled towards the protection of the forts and larger settlements east of the Blue Ridge Mountains. Crops were neglected and failed, and want was everywhere.

Another British commander, General John Forbes, was sent out to drive the French from Fort Duquesne, and Washington again accompanied the expedition, in the summer of 1758. This time, to everyone's surprise, there was no battle. The French had left the fort before the British arrived there, and before they went they had burned and destroyed everything they could not take with them. The British took possession, a sick, underfed, discouraged army, without even the satisfaction of a surrender ceremony and the capture of French flags and supplies. Washington was now regarded as a hero at Williamsburg, and although he wanted to retire from the army, the Governor urged him to remain at the frontier forts restoring order there.

Washington about this time had acquired Mount Vernon from the widow of his half-brother, and himself married a young widow named Martha Custis, who had two small children. In 1759 he left the army and took his seat as a Burgess in the Assembly at Williamsburg. All he desired

The French and Indians fired on Braddock's forces from behind rocks and trees

now was to become a family man and improve his acres on the Potomac. But the career which led to his becoming Commander-in-Chief of the American Army and the first President of the United States had already begun.

Soon the dauntless pioneers began to push westward again, into territory which still belonged to the Indians if not to the French. When we think of the perilous western frontier where the Indians and the wild animals waited in the dense forests, we remember Daniel Boone and Davy Crockett. Boone was about the same age as Washington, but he had had a very different kind of life. He grew up as a woodsman in the wild Yadkin River country in North Carolina, and about the time Washington retired to Mount Vernon Boone took his family into what became Kentucky. There he had many adventures and narrow escapes from death, and established a palisaded town called Boonesborough near what is now Frankfort. Davy Crockett was born much later, but was

Martha Custis was a young widow when she married George Washington

in time to see the wild early days of what is now Tennessee. He became a delegate to Congress and died at the Alamo in Texas in 1836.

These men became famous as Indian fighters and hunters, but there were many others whose names have not survived in history and legend. These unknowns also suffered the frontier hardships and dangers and stood their ground with their valiant wives and children against the constant threat of Indian massacre and death by starvation and winter cold if the meager crops failed or were destroyed.

Overland travel was unbelievably hard, for they must hack a way through dense forests to make a narrow road for their wagons loaded with simple household goods. They must cut timber to build weathertight cabins of logs with dirt floors, and they had to clear enough land of tree stumps and rocks to plant corn and potatoes and the precious seeds they brought with them. If their horses or cattle died it was almost impossible to replace them with others. Food—just enough food to keep them and their families alive from season to season—was a constant problem, and clothing for warmth and the least kind of comforts were valuable.

We can't help but wonder what restlessness or curiosity or desire for acres of their own drove these hardy people out from the seaboard settlements where life had begun to be reasonably civilized and safe, and the Indians were no longer a daily threat. Yet it seemed that as often as other families arrived and a little community grew up around them, men like Daniel Boone felt an itch to go farther, to push on westward into more solitude and danger which at that time seemed to stretch endlessly ahead of them. And we can't but pity their womenfolk for their bravery and loyalty, trying to make a home and bear their children without doctors or nursing and bring them up and teach them to read the Bible and write their names, in a wilderness where there

Indians were a constant threat on the lonely frontier

were no schools or regular teachers. Boys were often grown men before they could spell or sign their own names.

The trails followed the river valleys in the early days—into what is now West Virginia and Tennessee and Kentucky. Companies were formed to exploit all this unoccupied land, and to establish trading posts and communications with the older settlements behind. It was rather like the first beginnings when companies in England sent out the little ships to Roanoke and Jamestown. But now there was no ocean to cross—only the Blue Ridge and the Alleghenies, and the great dark forests which had never seen an ax.

The companies now included names recognized as American, like Washington, Mason, Carter, and Lee. With the first money he ever earned, as a boy surveyor, Washington had bought a tract of land up near Winchester which was then the western frontier of Virginia. Year by year he extended his holdings in the west until, as he grew older, he was able to sell some of it off again to help finance his loving care of Mount Vernon and his growing family responsibilities. When Thomas Jefferson was born at his father's place called Shadwell in 1743, "up country" from Tidewater society, it was at the edge of the wilderness. He built his own famous house, Monticello, nearby in 1769, and even then transportation between there and Williamsburg was still difficult. Monticello was one of the first big plantation mansions to lie beyond the riverbanks.

Soon after Braddock's defeat, Governor Dinwiddie had become old and ill and asked to be replaced. Francis Fauquier (pronounced Fawk-*eer*) arrived in Virginia in time to announce a peace treaty signed at Paris to end the Seven Years War on the Continent and an agreement with the French in America. France yielded its claim to all territory east of the Mississippi, except the city of New Orleans. The war had cost the British Government so much that under a new king, George III, they attempted to tax the American colonies for a share in the expense, which caused a storm of protest in America. The Virginia Assembly insisted that the right to tax Virginians belonged to them and not to the Parliament in London, where they were not represented. A series of resolutions was read against the so-called Stamp Act, which levied a tax on the stamp attached to all legal documents, and even required a stamp tax on newspapers, almanacs, and playing cards.

The spokesman for this first colonial resistance to taxation by Parliament was a young backwoods lawyer named Patrick Henry. His fiery oratory in the Virginia Assembly was interrupted by shocked cries of "Treason!" until he finished by saying, *"If this be treason make the most of it!"* This stirring scene at the Capitol took place in May, 1765, and is considered by some historians to be the first step

"If this be treason make the most of it!"
cried Patrick Henry to the Virginia Assembly

towards the rebellion against the King and Parliament which led to the Declaration of Independence at Philadelphia eleven years later.

Governor Fauquier, with great wisdom and moderation in the circumstances, prorogued, or suspended, the Assembly, so that the heated debates could not continue. He felt that Patrick Henry had gone much too far and should have time to cool off. The following year Parliament withdrew the Stamp Act without really enforcing it, though a tax on tea and some other articles in daily use was retained, in order to show the colonies that Parliament insisted on its right to tax them if it chose. It was, however, considered a back-down by the Ministry in London, and the end of the Stamp Act caused much rejoicing and celebration, not only in Williamsburg but in all the American colonies.

Governor Fauquier was given credit for handling a hot situation with tact and good humor. Thomas Jefferson, who was then a young law student at Williamsburg, said that Fauquier was the ablest man ever to hold the office of Governor. When Fauquier died in 1768 the whole colony mourned him, and he was buried with great ceremony in the north aisle of Bruton Church in Williamsburg, where his stone can be seen today. The *Gazette* published some verses in his honor, which read in part:

> If ever Virtue lost a friend sincere,
> If ever Sorrow claimed Virginia's tear,
> If ever Death a noble conquest made,
> 'Twas when Fauquier the debt of Nature paid.

The next man to govern Virginia for the King was a lucky choice, for to follow a man as beloved as Fauquier had been was not easy. Lord Botetourt (pronounced Botytot) was a genial bachelor, who gave wonderful parties at the Palace, and drove around in a magnificent coach with six white horses which he had brought with him from England. It was his democratic habit to go on foot through the Williamsburg streets in the warm summer evenings, accompanied by a servant carrying a lantern, and pause to chat with the people he met. His good nature and desire to keep the peace between the colony and the King made him popular, and his death after only two years was a great misfortune. He was buried in the College chapel, and a statue of him still stands on the little triangular green lawn in front of the College.

Things might have turned out differently if he had lived longer. But he was followed by Lord Dunmore, a bullheaded Scot who was chosen by the Ministry in London to reflect and enforce their growing determination to rule the headstrong American colonies. Meanwhile, from Massachusetts to South Carolina there was increasing resentment of interference from England with local affairs.

Lord Botetourt (left) was a genial bachelor who gave wonderful parties at the Palace. Lord Dunmore (right) was a tactless and hot-tempered governor

Dunmore brought with him his wife and family. His three sons became students at the College, and his three daughters were much courted by the Williamsburg gentlemen. Virginians were by now accustomed to liking their Governors, and welcomed the Dunmore family cordially. Dunmore surrounded himself with almost royal ceremony and grandeur, and was at once in conflict with the Burgesses in the Assembly over what they considered their own local business, which should be decided by local laws.

This was where the division in opinion began. Even in the Stamp Act, the London Parliament was thinking in terms of the whole British Empire, which included the American colonies—while at the same time the colonies on their side felt that as they were not represented in London they could not, or should not, be ruled and taxed from London. They objected to what they called injustice, and this feeling of resentment and persecution gradually turned into a desire for independence from the British Crown and a desire to rule themselves.

Virginia was not alone among the colonies in reaching this state of mind. In the north Massachusetts in particular was equally firm and much noisier about demanding its rights, and the Ministry in London sent troops to Massachusetts to put down the opposition and keep order, which brought the "redcoats" to Boston. Parliament did not quarter troops in Virginia, but was more roundabout there, attempting to control the Assembly through the Governor and by his authority. They backed him by sending some warships to lie in the York River.

Dunmore was the wrong man for this job, for unlike Fauquier and Botetourt he was tactless and hot-tempered and very jealous of his official position. In Boston there were riots and speech-making, and much ill-feeling grew up between the troops and the townsfolk. Early in 1770 a street brawl at the Customs House resulted in the death of five citizens when the soldiers fired on a disorderly mob. This was called the Boston Massacre, and was the first instance in the American colonies of bloodshed between people who were all of them English and all subjects of the same King.

Happily for Virginia, there were no "redcoats" on its soil. While Boston was boiling over, life went on much as usual in Williamsburg, with its lawn-parties and horseracing and balls at the Palace, where both men and women wore their hair powdered as was the formal fashion, and Colonel Washington wore the blue and scarlet uniform of the Virginia regiment which had fought with Braddock. But under the surface, distrust and dislike of Governor Dunmore were growing.

Early in 1773 news came that the British revenue ship *Gaspee*, which had been sent by the Ministry to collect the taxes, had been attacked and burned by the colonists in Rhode Island. If the men responsible for its destruction could be caught they were to be sent to England for trial. This meant that they would probably never be seen at home again, and a spirit of revolt began to simmer everywhere. At the Assembly in Williamsburg a resolution was introduced, calling for Committees of Correspondence to be organized for the purpose of collecting and circulating news of all such events in the sister colonies, and of the actions of the Ministry in England. In the days when newspapers were scarce and often weeks behind the events, and there were no regular news services to keep people informed, the founding of these private, independent information bureaus was an important step. Moreover, it made a link, or bond of union, among the widely scattered colonies and their leaders and spokesmen.

It was in this way that Williamsburg learned next of the event known as the Boston Tea Party. In December, 1773, a group of Boston citizens had disguised themselves as Indians and dumped a cargo of tea into the harbor as a protest against the tax which was laid on its sale. To punish Boston for this act, the Ministry ordered the port of Boston closed "by armed force," until with no shipping coming in or going out Boston would feel the pinch enough to apologize and pay for the tea. Boston of course refused, and called on the other colonies for support.

It happened that the Virginia Assembly was in session in May, 1774, when it received word of what was called the Boston Port Bill, sealing off the city. The Burgesses promptly passed Resolutions protesting this action against Boston, and set aside June 1 as "a day of fasting, humiliation, and prayer," to show sympathy for Massachusetts.

This harmless and peaceful display of disapproval by the Burgesses sent Dunmore into a rage, and he dismissed the Assembly, to prevent any further action of this kind. Certain leading members of it met the next day in the famous supper-room at the Raleigh Tavern, and sent messages to the Committees of Correspondence in the other twelve colonies advising them to appoint delegates from each colony to meet in "a general Congress" at some such place as Philadelphia, which was a fairly equal distance between north and south, "to deliberate on those general measures which the united interests of America may from time to time require."

This is the first appearance of that word "united," though "independence" was not yet being discussed. It was also the first recognition of "America" as a separate country from England, which was still thought of as "home" by most of the residents in America. And it is the first appearance of several men whose names alone were to become the symbols of new and enlightened ideas of justice and freedom and courage in the country called America.

August 1, 1774, was set as the date for a Convention at Williamsburg, for the main purpose of choosing Virginia's delegates to the first Congress at Philadelphia. Foremost among the men who rode into town for this meeting was George Washington of Mount Vernon on the Potomac. He was then forty-two years old, married to his Martha for fifteen years, and retired, forever he had supposed, from his boyhood army days on the frontier. He was a tall man, of great dignity and very few words, and he was admired by all in the little capital of Williamsburg. He found many of his old friends and fellow Burgesses already there, and they were glad to see him arrive.

One man was missing, to everyone's regret. Thomas Jefferson had fallen sick on the way in from his mountain home, and was forced to turn back. He had sent on in his place the text of a paper he had written, called "A Summary View of the Rights of British America." This document was read, discussed, and published as a pamphlet, and it contained many of the ideas its author included when he came to write the Declaration of Independence in 1776. Jefferson was thirty-one, and had a beautiful wife in delicate health and several children. He was tall and lanky, with sandy hair and a husky, untrained voice which prevented him from speaking effectively in the Assembly. He was a noteworthy scholar and a graduate of William and Mary College, and had played violin duets with Governor Fauquier, "neither of them very good." In 1768, before he married the widow of his friend Bathurst Skelton, he began to build the house he called Monticello on a hilltop in Albemarle County in the Charlottesville neighborhood—he was almost the only man of consequence in Virginia at this time who was not Tidewater born and bred. In 1774 he had been a Burgess and a lawyer for some four or five years.

The Convention at Williamsburg reached various important decisions. They agreed to Philadelphia as the place and September 5 as the date for the Congress, later to be called Continental. They chose seven delegates to represent Virginia there, and made out certain instructions for their guidance. No more British goods were to be imported into America, and tea in particular was banned if Boston was further punished for destroying the tea shipment in December, 1773. Loyal wives of distinguished patriots not only locked up their tea-caddies but soon took to wearing cotton and homespun dresses instead of imported silks and velvets.

The Speaker of the Virginia Assembly and Moderator, or President, of the Convention was Peyton Randolph, and he was chosen to head the Virginia delegates to Philadelphia. He was eleven years older than Washington, and had been a Burgess at the Virginia Assembly for ten years when Washington first took his seat there. Before that, Randolph had studied law, which was the "gentleman's" profession, at the Middle Temple in London. He was one of the few close friends of Washington, who often dined with him. Randolph had the same kind of noble presence and self-possession that always distinguished Washington. He was a large, genial man, who appeared—perhaps on purpose—to be lazy, but he carried great influence both in the Assembly and at Philadelphia, where he was also chosen to preside.

Since the Stamp Act crisis nearly ten years before, Peyton Randolph had changed completely from what was called the Tory attitude of loyalty to the British Crown and Ministry. He had developed a passionate belief in the rights and grievances of the colonists, and openly opposed inter-

Peyton Randolph (left) headed the Virginia delegation to the First Continental Congress, which included aristocratic Richard Henry Lee (below)

ference by the Ministry in matters of taxation, importation, and the trial of people whom the Ministry considered political offenders. This caused a tragic split in the Randolph family, for Peyton's brother John, like their father, was Tory to the backbone, and refused to accept Peyton's changeover to the colonial cause. But John's son Edmund went along with his childless Uncle Peyton, and became like a son to him. Edmund was named one of the Virginia delegation and accompanied Peyton to Philadelphia as the youngest member. He was twenty-one, dark, handsome, portly, a fine speaker with a lawyer's training.

Third on the list was Richard Henry Lee of the great Lee family, an aristocrat educated in England. He was the same age as Washington, and made formal speeches in a clear, musical voice as though he had practiced them in front of a mirror. Two more of Washington's friends on the Virginia team were the elderly Edmund Pendleton, a self-made lawyer who commanded a great deal of respect, and Richard Bland, "a learned and bookish man," who still hoped for some kind of agreement between the colonies and England.

In striking contrast to these fine gentlemen was Patrick Henry, the rather shabby country lawyer who, they said, "dressed like a parson," and wore a reddish wig which was often askew. But Henry was already famous in Virginia for his eloquence and his reckless insistence that the colonies should hold out against what he called tyranny.

The seventh man in the Virginia delegation was, of course, George Washington, who had always attended the Assembly faithfully, listened attentively, and never made speeches.

chapter 8

The First Step Towards Independence

The story of the First Continental Congress which met at Philadelphia in September, 1774, belongs to Pennsylvania. Another year and another Virginia Convention were to pass before the actual break with the mother country occurred. But this first meeting between the great men of all the colonies (except Georgia) was important as the beginning of the united resolve of 1776.

This September meeting brought together such widely different and opposite types of men as our Virginia friends and the two Massachusetts delegates, the city-bred John and Sam Adams of Boston. South Carolina sent Thomas Middleton and two of the famous Rutledges, who were the same kind of wealthy plantation owners as the Virginians. But distances were too great and transportation too poor for them ever to have met and exchanged their views except at Philadelphia.

This first Congress was notable for a speech by Patrick Henry, who on the second day expressed in his ringing tones the reason they were all there, when he startled them by saying, "I am not a Virginian! *I am an American!*" They were all Americans now, except for a few cautious holdouts who thought that everything was moving too fast.

Delegates to the First Continental Congress leaving Carpenter's Hall in Philadelphia

It might seem that when the Congress adjourned late in October it had accomplished very little besides talk. But they drew up and signed another petition which they sent to the King. In it they listed their grievances again and stated their intention to resist. Allowing for slow communications, they agreed that if a satisfactory answer was not received from England before May, 1775, they would meet again at Philadelphia and decide what to do next. As they disbanded towards their homes, many of them feared that things could only get worse, and they dreaded that Patrick Henry's reckless talk of an independent American state would make trouble for them all. Old friends quarrelled, and families like the Randolphs took opposite sides, and some stubborn Tories sold out, packed up their families, and sailed away to England, where their sympathies lay.

In Williamsburg the winter seemed to pass much as usual, in a lull before the storm, while they waited for the King's reply to the petition from Philadelphia. A date in March had been set for a second Virginia Convention to choose the delegates to the Second Continental Congress, which most people felt was sure to come.

The first delegation had been chosen at Williamsburg, but the Royal Governor was there, and a British battleship lay in the York River. To avoid Dunmore's rage, and its possible results of arrest or other unpleasantness for the delegates, they held the March Convention at Richmond in St. John's Church. This simple white frame building on one of Richmond's seven hills was smaller then, for it has been enlarged several times, but it was the largest meeting hall outside of Williamsburg, and the delegates assembled there.

Washington was of course present among most of the same men who had attended the First Congress, and he was of course chosen as delegate to the Second. There was one change, however. Peyton Randolph's position as Speaker of the House in Williamsburg obliged him to be there to try to keep the lid on Dunmore, and Thomas Jefferson, now recovered and present, was chosen to go to Philadelphia in Randolph's place. His wife was ill at Monticello, and always tried to hold him at her side. He wanted George Mason to take his place at Philadelphia, but Mason always refused to take any further part in politics. He had served one term in the Assembly at Williamsburg, the same year Washington first took his seat there. Mason's wife had recently died, leaving him with a large family of young children, and he almost never left his flourishing plantation which lay on the Potomac shore just below Mount Vernon. He was often consulted for his great learning and balanced judgment, and he exercised a quiet influence from his home at Gunston Hall. In 1774, in consultation with Washington, he had written out a declaration of rights called the Fairfax [County] Resolves, and many of his speeches and writings during the early 1770's seem to have been at the back of Jefferson's mind in July, 1776. The name of George Mason should never be forgotten among the more famous ones of his time.

In the summer of 1775, when recruiting had become pretty lively and men were hurrying to enlist, Mason presided at a local meeting of the Fairfax County Independent Company of Volunteers. They had adopted the blue and buff colors later chosen by Washington as the Continental uniform—though few of the common soldiers ever wore one, for lack of the funds to outfit them. On this occasion Mason said, "We came equals into this world, and equals we shall go out of it. All men are by nature born equally free and independent." These words now have a very familiar sound.

Mason was not present at Richmond during the March

Convention, and Jefferson unwillingly consented to go to Philadelphia. It was Patrick Henry who made the famous speech in the Church at Richmond. No exact record of Henry's oratory was ever kept. Certain phrases, however, made such an impression on his hearers that they were repeated over and again, so that we can almost hear them still, in his rather rasping, up-country accent, so different from the gentle Tidewater speech of his colleagues. Henry would have made a great actor, and he held his Richmond audience spellbound as he swept on to his stirring conclusion: "Is life so dear, or peace so sweet, as to be purchased at the price of chains and slavery? Forbid it, Almighty God! I know not what course others may take; but as for me, *give me liberty or give me death!*"

The next act in the great drama took place in Massachusetts, and was echoed at once in Virginia. The Royal Governor at Boston, Thomas Gage, was sending out detachments of soldiers to collect ammunition and weapons stored in the countryside by the colonists, and to break up the

Thomas Jefferson

George Mason

militia companies which were drilling everywhere around Boston. On the night of April 18, 1775, a larger British force than usual, about seven hundred men, left Boston secretly for Lexington and Concord, where they were to collect cannon and gunpowder. Two prominent members of the Massachusetts Assembly were known to be spending the night at Lexington. As soon as the British troops began embarking in small boats to cross the Charles River towards Cambridge and the march to Lexington, the Massachusetts Committee of Safety sent Paul Revere on his famous ride to rouse the countryside and warn Samuel Adams and John Hancock that they might be arrested. When the British arrived they were confronted on Lexington green by about seventy armed Minute Men, as the farmer soldiers were called. Shots were exchanged, and there were casualties on both sides. The British continued their march to Concord, while hundreds of colonial volunteers mustered to bar their way. There was another battle at Concord Bridge, and in a running fight the British force retreated into Boston. The militia chased them all the way, gathering strength and confidence as they went, and bottled the British up inside the town. This was the opening battle of the Revolution, two months before Bunker Hill.

News of the shooting at Lexington and Concord had not had time to reach Williamsburg when Governor Dunmore became alarmed by the decision of the Richmond Convention to raise the militia and "put the colony in a posture of defence." Dunmore suddenly sent a party of British marines from the warship to seize the weapons and powder stored in the little brick Magazine at Williamsburg. His move was successful, and the powder was carried on board the ship. Immediately, excited volunteers all along

Lord Dunmore seized weapons and powder stored in this brick Magazine at Williamsburg

the Tidewater gathered to march on the capital, occupy the Magazine, and demanded the powder back. Dunmore barricaded himself in the Palace, armed his servants, and threatened to raise the slave population to defend him. Peyton Randolph showed great presence of mind and authority, and by appearing personally on the green in front of the Palace he prevented an attack on it.

There was no battle in Virginia, thanks to Randolph's prompt action. But the shooting at Concord was not just a civilian mob against the British regulars, as the Boston Massacre had been. This Concord affair was between British soldiers and an armed force of Massachusetts farmers who considered themselves an army. This was war.

At Williamsburg the Governor had had a fright, and he agreed to pay for the powder, rather than give it back where it might be used against him. The volunteers went home satisfied that they had won a victory. And the Virginia delegates took the road to Philadelphia and the Second Congress.

chapter 9

The War Begins

The Second Continental Congress met on May 10, 1775, with almost the same membership as the first. The shooting at Lexington and Concord was fresh in their minds, when they reached Philadelphia. Washington wore his uniform this time, apparently as a sign of his willingness to serve in any way they wanted him to. Certainly he had no idea that he might be appointed Commander-in-Chief of the Continental Army, which was to happen the following month. He was the only man there in uniform, and almost the only man of any soldiering experience. Nevertheless, his letters show that the honor both surprised and dismayed him when it came.

The most notable addition to the Congress was the venerable Dr. Benjamin Franklin. He had recently returned from London where he had been acting as a sort of unofficial ambassador for the colonies. As soon as he got home to Philadelphia he was made a delegate for Pennsylvania.

It was mid-June before Jefferson arrived reluctantly to replace Peyton Randolph, who had his hands full at Williamsburg, because of the rising tide of anger among the people after the news of Lexington and Concord arrived there. At this second Congress Patrick Henry made no outstanding speeches, and he left there within a few weeks to become a colonel in the Virginia militia. But he was not a soldier by nature, and soon resigned his commission.

The Assembly session at Williamsburg came to a sudden end early in June, when Governor Dunmore in a rage removed himself and his family from the Palace to the British warship in the York River. He insisted that their lives were in danger from the rebellious colonists, after more trouble over arms and ammunion stored in the Magazine at Williamsburg. When he refused to return to the Capitol to sign bills and permit legislature which was important to the colony, the Burgesses declared that the Royal rule in Virginia had been abdicated, and the Assembly dissolved itself. Its members at once called another convention to discuss a new government and a plan of self-defense if they were attacked by the King's troops in support of Dunmore. The Governor was soon heard from again, as he began to make hit-and-run raids along the shore with his little fleet of armed ships, carrying off cattle and provisions, and urging the slaves to revolt and take up arms.

Meanwhile at Philadelphia Washington received a unanimous vote to command the amateur army which was forming itself throughout the colonies and would soon need a leader. Only two letters from Washington to his wife have survived. It is said that she burnt all the others shortly before she died, but these two escaped—perhaps because she realized even then what a gift to history they would be.

Both were written from Philadelphia at the time of his appointment to command the American army. They are important because they allow a rare glimpse into the heart of this great man, whose dignity and reserve have made him seem almost as cold and hard to know as his statues. But Washington was a family man, devoted to his wife, whom he always called Patsy, and he was always a kindly father to her two children by her first marriage, though he had none of his own.

His letter announcing to Martha the heavy new responsibility which had been laid on his shoulders by Congress began:

George Washington was devoted to his wife and her two children by her previous marriage

"*My Dearest:*

"I am now set down to write you on a subject which fills me with inexpressible concern, and this concern is greatly aggravated and increased when I reflect upon the uneasiness I know it will cause you. It has been determined in Congress that the whole army raised for the defence of the American cause shall be put under my care, and that it is necessary for me to proceed immediately to Boston to take upon me the command of it.

"You may believe me, my dear Patsy, when I assure you in the most solemn manner that, so far from seeking this appointment, I have used every endeavor in my power to avoid it, not only from my unwillingness to part with you and the family, but from a consciousness of its being a trust too great for my capacity; and that I should enjoy more real happiness in one month with you at home than I have the most distant prospect of finding abroad, if my stay were to be seven times seven years. But as it has been a kind of destiny that has thrown me upon this service, I shall hope that my undertaking it is designed to answer some good purpose. . ."

Washington's long letter to his wife ended with a homey sort of postscript:

"Since writing the above, I have received your letter of the 15th and have got two suits of what I was told was the prettiest muslin. I wish it may please you. It cost 50 shillings a suit, that is, 20 shillings a yard."

In the midst of the Congress meetings and the military preparations going on all around him, Washington had taken the time and trouble to go to a shop and choose the prettiest material he could find to send to his wife for new dresses.

It is difficult to imagine what the outcome would have been if Washington had refused, or if someone else had been chosen as Commander-in-Chief. It was Washington's own courage and firmness of purpose, and the strong personal magnetism of his tall, dignified presence which inspired the devotion of his troops, as much as it was his military genius which carried the army under his command to victory. It required courage of another sort, too, besides his coolness under gunfire which had already been demonstrated many times over. Everyone knew that if he failed, and was captured or was forced to surrender, he was guilty of treason against the British King, and treason in those days was punishable by death by hanging. Not only Washington himself, but many of his officers and many members of the Congress would have been liable to trial and execution in England if the Revolution had failed.

At least one man, John Hancock of Massachusetts, did want Washington's job as Commander-in-Chief, and was vain enough to think he could do it as well as Washington could—but Hancock's ill health and lack of experience on a battlefield were against him. He remained in Philadelphia as President of the Congress after Peyton Randolph's death left that post vacant—one to which Hancock was much better suited than to lead troops in the field.

The day before he left Philadelphia to take charge of the ragged, undisciplined army which had been encamped outside Boston ever since the fight at Concord in April, the dramatic news of a battle at Bunker Hill reached the Congress. The Americans had run out of powder in the middle of the fight, after heavy losses on both sides. But the green American troops had behaved well against the trained British regulars, and had caused such slaughter among them that the white buckskin breeches of the British General William Howe were stained with the blood of his wounded officers, though Howe himself was not bleeding.

Washington saw that the war was not going to wait for him now. On the morning of June 23 he dashed off a last note to Martha before setting out for Boston.

"*My Dearest:*

"As I am within a few minutes of leaving this city, I could not think of departing from it without dropping you a line, especially as I do not know whether it will be within my power to write you again till I get to the camp at Boston. I go fully trusting in that Providence which has been more bountiful to me than I deserve, and in full confidence of a happy meeting with you in the Fall. I have no time to add more, as I am surrounded with company come to take leave of me. I retain an unalterable affection for you which neither time nor distance can change. Conclude me with the utmost truth and sincerity, Your entire, GEORGE WASHINGTON."

But by the time fall came, the Americans realized they were in for a long war. Washington had set up his headquarters at Cambridge outside Boston and still held the British bottled up in the town, because he had not enough trained men or enough ammunition to force them out of it. Martha travelled all the way from Mount Vernon to Cambridge to spend the winter months with him, as she was to do every single winter of the war, even at Valley Forge. But it was six years before he saw Mount Vernon again, on his way to Yorktown.

Early in the autumn of 1775, while Washington was deadlocked at Boston, Dunmore raised the Royal standard at Norfolk, Virginia, and proclaimed martial law, which meant that all civil liberties gave way to the harsh rule of the army, which began to plunder and destroy. He tried to raise the Indians and the slaves against the colonists by offering them weapons and food if they would join him.

To prevent the loss of their precious stores and end Dunmore's reign of terror, the militia of the countryside roundabout Norfolk were called to arms under Colonel William Woodford, a veteran of the French and Indian War. Dunmore had fortified himself at Great Bridge on the Elizabeth River near the North Carolina border below Norfolk. He had by now collected a ragged following of Negroes and Loyalists, which was another name for Tories, besides the troops from his ships, and was at his old game of seizing and destroying food supplies and ammunition collected by the Virginians for their own use. Woodford advanced to the other end of the long bridge, which was approached at each end by a paved causeway built across a marsh. Here he placed himself between Dunmore and the threatened supplies by camping near a church at his end of the bridge and constructing breastworks to protect his men.

Dunmore stayed safe in the rear, while his force was led by a Captain Fordyce. To attack Woodford and capture the stores, Fordyce had to march his men six abreast across the narrow causeway leading to the bridge. Woodford's militia, who were all good marksmen, had only to hold their fire until the British came close enough so that the first volley mowed down the front men in the column. They rallied and came on, and received a second murderous volley, which killed Fordyce—there were fourteen bullets in his body. The survivors fled back to Norfolk. The only casualty among the Americans was one man slightly wounded. Dunmore lost more than sixty.

This half-forgotten skirmish was the first bloodshed on Virginia soil in the Revolution, and could be compared to the Lexington and Concord fight in Massachusetts the previous April. Dunmore withdrew his soldiers to his ships, and deserted the Negroes and country people who had joined him. He left them without provisions or protection of any kind, and many of them died of exposure and hunger. Woodford took possession of Norfolk, and from there fired

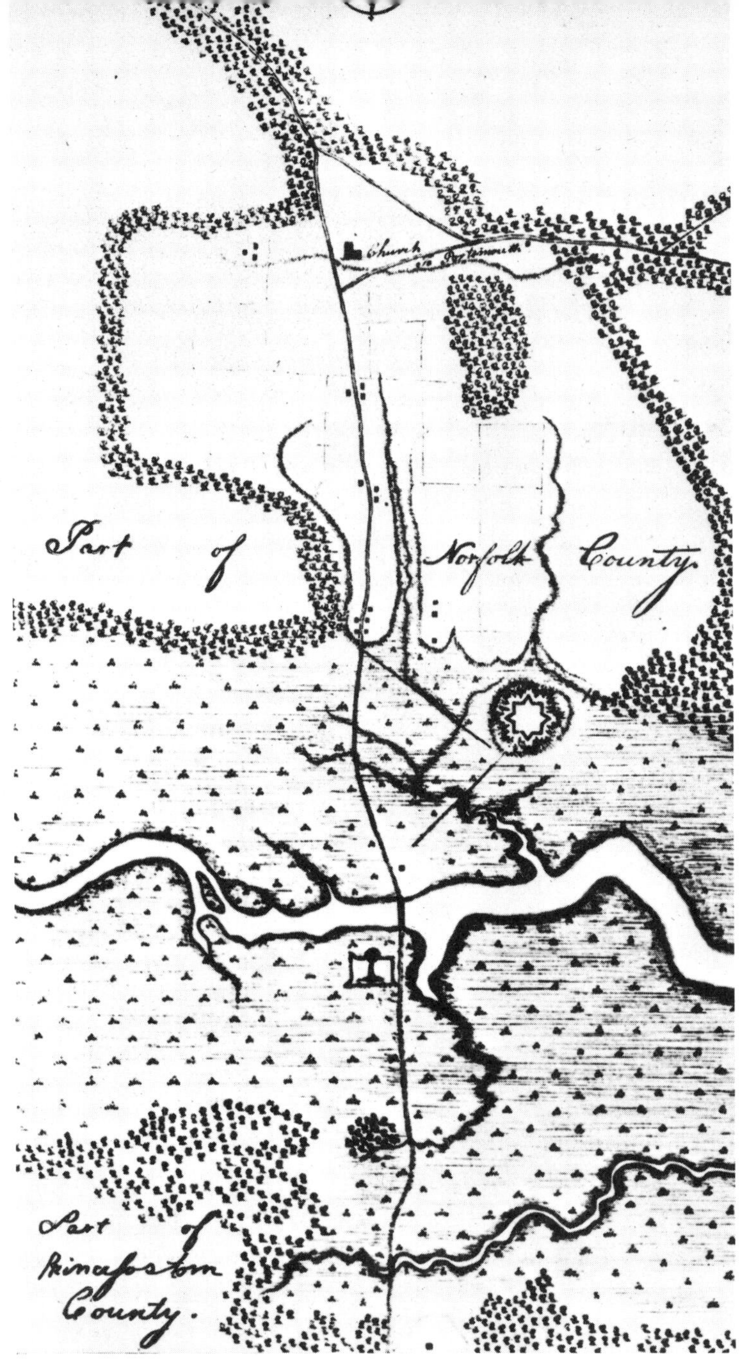

An early map of Great Bridge on the Elizabeth River, site of the first bloodshed on Virginia soil in the Revolution. The line through the center of the map represents the causeway that crossed the marsh on either side of the river

on Dunmore's ships which lay off shore. Food soon ran short on the ships, and Dunmore turned his cannon on the town until he set it on fire. This destroyed many homes as well as the docks and warehouses, and caused great suffering to the inhabitants in the January weather.

Finally Dunmore took his ships into the Chesapeake and landed on an island there and began to fortify it. When he was driven from there by gunfire from the shore, he took his battered little fleet to New York and joined the British there in the summer of 1776. The Americans landed on the island after he had departed, and were horrified at what they found. Dunmore had left many of his wounded untended and in dreadful condition, and had only half buried his dead. It was a disgraceful end to British glory in Virginia.

The British evacuated Boston in March, 1776, and Washington moved his army to New York, where the next British attack was expected. In May a British fleet fired on Charleston, South Carolina, which defended itself so vigorously from its forts along the shore that the British were forced to withdraw to New York.

This was open warfare, and the Convention at Williamsburg realized that now there could be no turning back, even though some conservative men at Philadelphia still hoped to arrange some kind of agreement with the King and his Ministry. Delegates to the Williamsburg Convention from various counties had been instructed to present resolutions "to abjure any allegiance to his Britannic Majesty, and bid him a good night forever." Several resolutions were accordingly drafted by the Convention, which directed the Virginia delegates at Philadelphia to move that the Congress there should "declare the United Colonies to be free and independent states," with Virginia's consent to such a declaration.

Furthermore, George Mason at Williamsburg drew up a

Declaration of Rights and a Plan of Government for Virginia, which was actually the first Constitution of an independent state in America.

Therefore, when Richard Henry Lee stood up before the Congress at Philadelphia and read the Virginia resolutions for independence, Virginia, which had been the first colony, was already in existence as the first state of the new United States of America. Patrick Henry was elected the first American Governor of Virginia, and moved into the Palace with his family. It was noticed that at this time he began to dress better, and even got himself a fine new cloak with a scarlet lining, and a new wig.

The Virginia resolutions were read to the Congress by Richard Henry Lee on May 15, 1776, and were heard with dismay by some of the delegates from other colonies. Many welcomed them, especially John Adams from Massachusetts. Congress appointed a committee to draft another declaration to represent the beliefs and intentions of the whole body. Most of this work was done by Thomas Jefferson in his modest lodgings, working alone by candlelight, racking his brains for phrases and expressions which would have come easier to him in his library at Monticello. His document was read and debated by Congress for several days until on July 4, 1776, the Declaration of Independence was voted unanimously, and all the bells of Philadelphia began to peal, as the new nation was born.

George Wythe, Richard Henry Lee, Thomas Jefferson, Benjamin Harrison, Thomas Nelson, Jr., Francis Lightfoot Lee, and Carter Braxton signed the Declaration of Independence for Virginia. Their signatures may be found in the third column

IN CONGRESS, JULY 4, 1776.

The unanimous Declaration of the thirteen united States of America,

When in the Course of human events, it becomes necessary for one people to dissolve the political bands which have connected them with another, and to assume among the powers of the earth, the separate and equal station to which the Laws of Nature and of Nature's God entitle them, a decent respect to the opinions of mankind requires that they should declare the causes which impel them to the separation. —— We hold these truths to be self-evident, that all men are created equal, that they are endowed by their Creator with certain unalienable Rights, that among these are Life, Liberty and the pursuit of Happiness. — That to secure these rights, Governments are instituted among Men, deriving their just powers from the consent of the governed, — That whenever any Form of Government becomes destructive of these ends, it is the Right of the People to alter or to abolish it, and to institute new Government, laying its foundation on such principles and organizing its powers in such form, as to them shall seem most likely to effect their Safety and Happiness. Prudence, indeed, will dictate that Governments long established should not be changed for light and transient causes; and accordingly all experience hath shewn, that mankind are more disposed to suffer, while evils are sufferable, than to right themselves by abolishing the forms to which they are accustomed. But when a long train of abuses and usurpations, pursuing invariably the same Object evinces a design to reduce them under absolute Despotism, it is their right, it is their duty, to throw off such Government, and to provide new Guards for their future security. — Such has been the patient sufferance of these Colonies; and such is now the necessity which constrains them to alter their former Systems of Government. The history of the present King of Great Britain is a history of repeated injuries and usurpations, all having in direct object the establishment of an absolute Tyranny over these States. To prove this, let Facts be submitted to a candid world. —— He has refused his Assent to Laws, the most wholesome and necessary for the public good. —— He has forbidden his Governors to pass Laws of immediate and pressing importance, unless suspended in their operation till his Assent should be obtained; and when so suspended, he has utterly neglected to attend to them. —— He has refused to pass other Laws for the accommodation of large districts of people, unless those people would relinquish the right of Representation in the Legislature, a right inestimable to them and formidable to tyrants only. —— He has called together legislative bodies at places unusual, uncomfortable, and distant from the depository of their public Records, for the sole purpose of fatiguing them into compliance with his measures. —— He has dissolved Representative Houses repeatedly, for opposing with manly firmness his invasions on the rights of the people. —— He has refused for a long time, after such dissolutions, to cause others to be elected; whereby the Legislative powers, incapable of Annihilation, have returned to the People at large for their exercise; the State remaining in the mean time exposed to all the dangers of invasion from without, and convulsions within. —— He has endeavoured to prevent the population of these States; for that purpose obstructing the Laws for Naturalization of Foreigners; refusing to pass others to encourage their migrations hither, and raising the conditions of new Appropriations of Lands. —— He has obstructed the Administration of Justice, by refusing his Assent to Laws for establishing Judiciary powers. —— He has made Judges dependent on his Will alone, for the tenure of their offices, and the amount and payment of their salaries. —— He has erected a multitude of New Offices, and sent hither swarms of Officers to harrass our people, and eat out their substance. —— He has kept among us, in times of peace, Standing Armies without the Consent of our legislatures. —— He has affected to render the Military independent of and superior to the Civil power. —— He has combined with others to subject us to a jurisdiction foreign to our constitution, and unacknowledged by our laws; giving his Assent to their Acts of pretended Legislation: —— For Quartering large bodies of armed troops among us: —— For protecting them, by a mock Trial, from punishment for any Murders which they should commit on the Inhabitants of these States: —— For cutting off our Trade with all parts of the world: —— For imposing Taxes on us without our Consent: —— For depriving us in many cases, of the benefits of Trial by Jury: —— For transporting us beyond Seas to be tried for pretended offences —— For abolishing the free System of English Laws in a neighbouring Province, establishing therein an Arbitrary government, and enlarging its Boundaries so as to render it at once an example and fit instrument for introducing the same absolute rule into these Colonies: —— For taking away our Charters, abolishing our most valuable Laws, and altering fundamentally the Forms of our Governments: —— For suspending our own Legislatures, and declaring themselves invested with power to legislate for us in all cases whatsoever. —— He has abdicated Government here, by declaring us out of his Protection and waging War against us. —— He has plundered our seas, ravaged our Coasts, burnt our towns, and destroyed the lives of our people. —— He is at this time transporting large Armies of foreign Mercenaries to compleat the works of death, desolation and tyranny, already begun with circumstances of Cruelty & perfidy scarcely paralleled in the most barbarous ages, and totally unworthy the Head of a civilized nation. —— He has constrained our fellow Citizens taken Captive on the high Seas to bear Arms against their Country, to become the executioners of their friends and Brethren, or to fall themselves by their Hands. —— He has excited domestic insurrections amongst us, and has endeavoured to bring on the inhabitants of our frontiers, the merciless Indian Savages, whose known rule of warfare, is an undistinguished destruction of all ages, sexes and conditions. In every stage of these Oppressions We have Petitioned for Redress in the most humble terms: Our repeated Petitions have been answered only by repeated injury. A Prince, whose character is thus marked by every act which may define a Tyrant, is unfit to be the ruler of a free people. Nor have We been wanting in attentions to our Brittish brethren. We have warned them from time to time of attempts by their legislature to extend an unwarrantable jurisdiction over us. We have reminded them of the circumstances of our emigration and settlement here. We have appealed to their native justice and magnanimity, and we have conjured them by the ties of our common kindred to disavow these usurpations, which, would inevitably interrupt our connections and correspondence. They too have been deaf to the voice of justice and of consanguinity. We must, therefore, acquiesce in the necessity, which denounces our Separation, and hold them, as we hold the rest of mankind, Enemies in War, in Peace Friends.

We, therefore, the Representatives of the united States of America, in General Congress, Assembled, appealing to the Supreme Judge of the world for the rectitude of our intentions, do, in the Name, and by Authority of the good People of these Colonies, solemnly publish and declare, That these United Colonies are, and of Right ought to be Free and Independent States; that they are Absolved from all Allegiance to the British Crown, and that all political connection between them and the State of Great Britain, is and ought to be totally dissolved; and that as Free and Independent States, they have full Power to levy War, conclude Peace, contract Alliances, establish Commerce, and to do all other Acts and Things which Independent States may of right do. —— And for the support of this Declaration, with a firm reliance on the protection of divine Providence, we mutually pledge to each other our Lives, our Fortunes and our sacred Honor.

John Hancock

Button Gwinnett
Lyman Hall
Geo Walton.

Wm Hooper
Joseph Hewes,
John Penn
Edward Rutledge 1.
Thos Heyward Junr.
Thomas Lynch Junr.
Arthur Middleton

Samuel Chase
Wm Paca
Thos Stone
Charles Carroll of Carrollton
George Wythe
Richard Henry Lee
Th Jefferson
Benja Harrison
Thos Nelson jr.
Francis Lightfoot Lee
Carter Braxton

Robt Morris
Benjamin Rush
Benja Franklin
John Morton
Geo Clymer
Jas Smith
Geo Taylor
James Wilson
Geo Ross
Caesar Rodney
Geo Read
Thos M'Kean

Wm Floyd
Phil Livingston
Frans Lewis
Lewis Morris
Richd Stockton
Jno Witherspoon
Fras Hopkinson
John Hart
Abra Clark

Josiah Bartlett
Wm Whipple
Saml Adams
John Adams
Robt Treat Paine
Elbridge Gerry
Step Hopkins
William Ellery
Roger Sherman
Samel Huntington
Wm Williams
Oliver Wolcott
Matthew Thornton

Bibliography

BRIERLY, E., *Streets of Old New York.* New York: Hastings House, 1953.

BURNETT, E., *The Continental Congress.* New York: Macmillan, 1941.

CAMPBELL, C., *History of the Virginia Colony.* Philadelphia: Lippincott, 1860.

CHATTERTON, E.K., *Captain John Smith.* New York: Harpers, 1927.

FISKE, J., *Old Virginia and Her Neighbors.* New York: Houghton Mifflin, 1925.

FITHIAN, PHILIP, *Journal and Letters.* Ed. H. Farish. Colonial Williamsburg, 1957.

FREEMAN, DOUGLAS SOUTHALL, *George Washington.* 7 vols. New York: Scribners, 1950–57.

GOODWIN, R., *Williamsburg in Virginia.* Colonial Williamsburg, 1940.

HAWTHORNE, H., *Williamsburg.* New York: Appleton-Century, 1941.

HILL, H., *George Mason.* Cambridge, Mass.: Harvard University Press, 1938.

HOWE, H., *Collections of Virginia History.* Henry Howe, 1847.

HOWISON, R., *History of Virginia.* Carey & Hart, 1848.

KIBLER, J.L., *Colonial Virginia Shrines.* Garrett & Massie, 1936.

LOSSING, BENSON, *Pictorial Handbook of the Revolution.* New York: Harper's, 1855.

MORGAN, E.S., *Virginians at Home.* Colonial Williamsburg, 1952.

MORTON, R.L., *Colonial Virginia.* Colonial Williamsburg, 1960.

SMITH, BRADFORD, *Captain John Smith.* Philadelphia: Lippincott, 1953.

SNOWDEN, W.H., *Some Old Landmarks of Virginia.* Philadelphia: Lippincott, 1894.

TYLER, L.G., *Cradle of the Republic.* Whittet and Shepperson, 1900.

Virginia Cavalcade (quarterly). Virginia State Library, Richmond.

George Washington's Diaries, ed. J. Fitzpatrick. New York: Houghton Mifflin, 1925.

WASHBURN, W.E., *Governor and Rebel.* Chapel Hill: University of North Carolina Press, 1957.

WATSON, ELKANAH, *Men and Times of the Revolution.* Dana, 1856.

WILSTACH, PAUL, *Tidewater Virginia.* New York: Doubleday Page, 1929.

YONGE, S., *Site of Old Jamestown.* L. H. Jenkins, 1936.

Important Dates

1492—Columbus discovers the West Indies.
1577—Drake's voyage around the world.
1587—First settlement at Roanoke.
1607—First settlement at Jamestown, Virginia.
Smith saved by Pocahontas.
1608—Newport brings First and Second Supply to Jamestown.
First Jamestown fire.
Mistress Forrest and Ann Burroughs arrive in Second Supply.
Ann Burroughs married at Jamestown church, in first Virginia wedding.
1609—Newport, Somers, and Gates shipwrecked on Bermuda.
Remnants of fleet with Third Supply arrive at Jamestown.
Smith returns to England.
1609–10—The Starving Time at Jamestown.
Newport, Gates, and Somers arrive from Bermuda, decide to abandon Jamestown settlement.
1610—Lord Delaware arrives in June. Jamestown is saved.
1611—Delaware returns to England, ill.
Colony deteriorates under Percy's rule.
1612—John Rolfe begins cultivation of tobacco.
1613—Pocahontas arrives at Jamestown as Argall's prisoner.
1614—Pocahontas marries Rolfe at Jamestown church.
1615—Birth of son to Pocahontas and Rolfe.
1616—Pocahontas and Rolfe accompany Dale to England.
1617—Pocahontas dies in England. Rolfe returns to America.
1618—Death of the Powhatan.
1619—First bride-ship arrives.
First Negroes brought in by Dutch trader.
First Assembly meets at Jamestown under new charter.
Colony expanding beyond fortifications.
1621—Governor Wyatt arrives.

1622—Indian massacre on Good Friday. Three hundred fifty settlers murdered at their homes outside Jamestown area.
1623—Plague arrives in ship from England.
1624—King James I dissolves London Company and takes personal rule of Virginia Colony, with Governors appointed by him. Virginia Assembly allowed to continue.
1625—Charles I succeeds James I in England.
Palisade built above Middle Plantation. Colony expanding up the riverbanks outside Jamestown area.
1639—First brick church built at Jamestown.
State House begun.
1642—Governor Berkeley arrives.
1649—Charles I executed in England.
Berkeley retires to Green Spring.
1650–60—Commonwealth rule in England.
Cavalier families find refuge in Virginia.
1660—After Cromwell's death Berkeley resumes as Governor of Virginia Colony under Charles II.
1665–73—England at war with Holland off and on, hurts trade.
Berkeley's growing misrule causes discontent at Jamestown.
Indians harassing frontier settlements.
1676—Nathaniel Bacon leads rebellion against Berkeley.
Second Jamestown fire.
Bacon dies of fever at the age of 29.
1677—Berkeley holds trials and executions at Green Spring.
Charles sends commission to govern Virginia, recalls Berkeley.
1677–88—Succession of minor Royal Governors.
Jamestown rebuilt.
1686—James II succeeds Charles II in England.
1688—William and Mary succeed James II.
1690—Governor Nicholson arrives.
1696—College of William and Mary founded at Middle Plantation.
1698—Third Jamestown fire.
1699—Capital removed to Middle Plantation after ninty-two years at Jamestown.
New town laid out and called Williamsburg.
1700—First commencement exercises at William and Mary.
1702—Queen Anne succeeds William III in England.
1710—Governor Spotswood arrives.
Palace at Williamsburg finished by Governor Spotswood.
1714—Queen Anne succeeded by George I.

1727—Governor Gooch arrives.
George II succeeds George I.

1752—Governor Dinwiddie arrives.

1754—George Washington sent to "remonstrate" with the French on the Ohio.
Washington defeated at Fort Necessity.

1755—Braddock leads expedition to the Monongahela. Washington assigned to his Staff.
Braddock defeated and killed.

1758—Forbes expedition to Fort Duquesne, accompanied by Washington, finds French have departed.
Governor Fauquier arrives.

1759—Washington marries Mrs. Custis and retires from the army to live at Mount Vernon.

1765—Stamp Act introduced by Parliament.
Opposition to Stamp Act in Virginia led by Patrick Henry.

1766—Stamp Act repealed by Parliament, leaving tax on tea.

1769—Governor Botetourt arrives after Fauquier's death.

1772—Governor Dunmore follows Botetourt.

1773—Boston Tea Party.

1774—Boston Port Bill. Dunmore dismisses Virginia Assembly.
Committees of Correspondence established.
First Continental Congress at Philadelphia.

1775—Richmond Convention.
Patrick Henry's speech on "liberty or death."
Apr. 19. Battle at Lexington and Concord in Massachusetts.
May 10. Second Continental Congress at Philadelphia.
June 15. Washington appointed Commander-in-Chief by Congress at Philadelphia.
June 17. Battle of Bunker Hill.
Dec. 9. Battle at Great Bridge, Virginia.
Dec. 11. Dunmore proclaims martial law in Virginia.

1776—Jan. 1. Dunmore burns Norfolk, Virginia.
Mar. 17. British evacuate Boston; Washington takes possession.
June 7. Richard Henry Lee introduces Resolutions for Independence at Philadelphia.
June 11. Jefferson at Philadelphia writes Declaration of Independence.
July 4. Declaration of Independence adopted.

Places To Visit

Readers may enjoy visiting the places below.

ALEXANDRIA could be called Washington's hometown. As a boy he helped to survey the site, and as a married man he maintained a small house there, and often attended *Christ Church,* where his family pew is marked with a silver plate.

Carlyle House, in North Fairfax Street, was built in 1752, and served as General Braddock's headquarters before his march to the Monongahela in 1755. Washington's first meeting with the General was said to have taken place here, as the Carlyles were his friends. The house is furnished and open to visitors at a small fee.

Gadsby's Tavern, Royal and Cameron Streets, also dating from 1752, has been much restored. This was the scene of the Alexandria dancing assemblies, often attended by Washington and his family, and the political meetings before the Revolution. The adoption of the new Constitution was celebrated here in 1788. The tavern is furnished and open to visitors at a small fee.

The Old Apothecary's Shop, in South Fairfax Street, has been furnished with the bottles and pestles of its period and is open to view.

Still standing but not often shown are many old houses which once belonged to Washington's friends, Dr. Craik, Dr. Dick, William Ramsay, and Lord Fairfax. A visit to Alexandria should always include a stroll through the streets of the old part of town, below the modern business district.

CAPE HENRY, at the lower end of the Chesapeake Bay, has a park and lighthouse marking the site of the first landing of the Jamestown colonists.

FREDERICKSBURG. John Smith visited this site in 1608 on one of his early explorations, but the town was not established until 1671.

The Rising Sun Tavern is said to have been built by George

Washington's brother Charles about 1760 and is furnished in the period and open to view.

Kenmore, the magnificent home built for Washington's sister Betty by her husband Fielding Lewis about 1752, has been beautifully restored and furnished with many original pieces, and should be seen.

The Mary Washington House lies behind Kenmore with a path through the garden, and is where Washington's mother lived during the latter part of her life, under Betty's care.

Hugh Mercer's Apothecary Shop, Amelia and Caroline Streets, was kept by one of Washington's close friends, and has a small back room where private meetings are supposed to have been held.

JAMESTOWN. The river tides have eaten away much of the original island as it was first seen by the colonists in 1607. In 1934 the National Park Service purchased the site and a sea wall now protects what remains of the acreage. At the time of the 350th anniversary of the first landing, the triangular fort and thatched cabins of the early settlement were carefully reconstructed as a part of the Jamestown Festival, and are well worth a visit. The Museum contains relics found during excavations on the old site. The only original structure remaining is the brick church tower which is part of the fourth or fifth church erected by the colonists about 1639 and repaired after the Bacon Rebellion. The churchyard contains a number of old graves with dilapidated headstones.

MONTICELLO, two miles southeast of Charlottesville, was the mountain home of Thomas Jefferson, which he designed and built beginning about 1770, and to which he retired after the Presidency and where he died. It has passed through many hands, but has now been restored and furnished by the Thomas Jefferson Memorial Association and is open daily, at a small fee.

MOUNT VERNON. Washington's beloved home on the Potomac is the most rewarding experience any traveller can have. After his death there in 1799 it was inherited by his nephew, and then another nephew, and was in a sad state of disrepair when it was purchased in 1858 by the Mount Vernon Ladies' Association, an organization of women dedicated to its preservation. In the possession of this Association the Mansion has been carefully repaired and furnished and many of its original objects and furniture pieces have been returned to their places in its rooms. Washington's bedroom, where he died, is almost certainly as he saw it last. The gardens are superb. The grounds and the Mansion house are open every day in the year from 9 A.M. until dusk, at a small fee.

RICHMOND. Although Captain Newport and John Smith ascended the James River as far as the site of Richmond, there was no permanent settlement here until in 1733 a town was laid out at a trading post which dated from 1637. In 1779, after the invasion of the South by the British army, the capital was moved up the river from Williamsburg to Richmond.

St. John's Church on Broad Street was the scene of the Virginia Convention in 1775, where Patrick Henry made his "liberty or death" speech.

WAKEFIELD. On Pope's Creek below Mount Vernon, the site of the house where George Washington was born is now occupied by a fine reconstruction of a plantation house of the period. No plan or picture of the original house exists, but the foundation remained to determine the general size and layout of the birthplace. The furnishings are of the right period, and it is well worth a visit. The old Washington family burial plot is nearby. Washington is buried at Mount Vernon and his mother near Fredericksburg. The house is open to view at a small fee.

WESTOVER. On the James River bank near Charles City. One of the great plantation houses, ancestral home of the Byrd family, built about 1755. It is privately owned and open only during Garden Week, in the Spring.

WILLIAMSBURG. The second capital city of Virginia, after Jamestown was abandoned in 1699, when the settlement known as the Middle Plantation became the seat of the government. The College of William and Mary was founded here in 1693. In 1926 the restoration of Colonial Williamsburg was undertaken by John D. Rockefeller, Jr., after painstaking research, and many millions have been spent on the excavation and restoration of the town's original aspect. Many of the old houses remained, and needed only maintenance and repair. The public buildings, like the Capitol, the Palace, and the Raleigh Tavern, had disappeared after fires, and had to be entirely reconstructed. The work is still going on. A detailed tour with costumed guides is available at a fee, and eighteenth-century meals are served at several inns. The Rockefeller Foundation has provided excellent accommodation at the luxurious Tavern and Inn, and motels have been built on the outskirts of the town, which now presents its original colonial aspect.

WINCHESTER. At the head of the Shenandoah Valley. The first survey of the site was made by George Washington as a boy of sixteen, on his first job for Lord Fairfax. His first military experience occurred here at Fort Loudoun, whose old earthwork remains at North Loudoun Street. A small building supposed to have been his headquarters during the construction of the fort is shown in Braddock Street.

YORKTOWN, first settled about 1630, became an official port town about 1680. The National Park Service has restored or reconstructed the 1781 fortifications and battlefield sites, which figured in the siege which was the virtual end of the Revolution. Cornwallis surrendered here to Washington and the supporting French army under Rochambeau. The *Moore House,* where the terms of surrender were drawn up, has been restored and is shown. The *Museum* has many relics of the siege, and the *Swan Tavern* has been reconstructed to its 1719 aspect. The *Nelson House,* which was occupied by Cornwallis as his headquarters, still shows a cannonball received in its brick wall during the siege. Built in 1740, it is now privately owned, but admission to house and garden can sometimes be obtained by a small fee.

Times and admission prices may change without notice.

Index